UNITT'S

Canadian Price Guide
to
Antiques
&
Collectables
Book
Fifteen

PETER UNITT AND ANNE WORRALL

Fitzhenry & Whiteside

AN ORIGINAL CANADIAN PUBLICATION

© 1993 - Fitzhenry & Whiteside

Canadian Cataloguing in Publication Data
The National Library of Canada has catalogued
this serial as follows:

Unitt, Doris, 1909-1978
  Unitt's Canadian price guide to antiques and
collectables

Book 1-   1968-
Vols. 1-7 prepared by Doris and Peter Unitt;
vols. 8-15 by Peter Unitt and Anne Worrall.
ISSN 0315-2383
ISBN 1-55041-169-1 (Bk. 15)

1. Collectors and collecting – Periodicals.
I. Unitt, Peter, 1914-   . II. Worrall, Anne.
III. Title.

NK1125.U6   745.1'0971   C75-033303-0

Printed and Bound in Canada

INTRODUCTION

Our price guides are compiled with the aid of information from many sources: antique shows, auctions, collectors and dealers. We have always looked for fresh material and the following new categories are featured in Price Guide 15: glass cigarette containers, sewing items, black collectables, radios, and jukeboxes. We hope you find them interesting.

It has often been remarked that dealers' prices are high, and sometimes they are, but it should be borne in mind that they have to compete with the general public at auctions, rent has to be paid for stores and/or stands at shows and travel is costly. Furniture and other items have to be restored and refinished, adding to the final selling price.

Anyone who has bought and sold antiques and collectables for a living or to augment income knows that it is a hazardous venture requiring capital, knowledge, and experience, combined with the patience and fortitude to survice difficult times. The last couple of years have been a true test of those qualities.

Collectors and dealers have always been generous with their time and knowledge and our guides would not be possible without their help. Our thanks to all who, knowingly or unknowling, have assisted.

A special 'thank you' to the following, we could not manage without you:

Lawrence & Jean Hartnell
Black Shutter Antiques
Stayner, Ontario

Bruce Carnall
Peterborough, Ontario

Peter Marshall
The Clock Doctor
Toronto, Ontario

Al & Karen Boswell
Cookie Jars North
Collingwood, Ontario

John Dunbar
Peterborough, Ontario

John Fraser
Fraser's Furniture Restoration
& Antiques
Peterborough, Ontario

Ruth Camken
Golden Orchard Antiques
Mississauga, Ontario

Edith & Doug Hacking
Hacking's Antiques
Mississauga, Ontario

Vera & Allan Fraser
Lamplighter Antiques
Pike Bay, Ontario

Nick Langston
Langmar Antiques
Locust Hill, Ontario

Doug Langs
Strathroy, Ontario

Dorothy & Wes Eardley
Little Barn Antiques
Cavan, Ontario

Jack Marsden
Cobourg, Ontario

Richard Crawford & Ken MacKay
Past Tyme Antiques
Peterborough, Ontario

Sean & Patty George
Patty George Antiques
Moorefield, Ontario

Sue & Ray Cobbing
Ray Cobbing Antiques & Collectables
Morganstown, Ontario

Randy Reddick
Oshawa, Ontario

Richard Rumi
Richard Rumi & Company
Mississauga, Ontario

Joy Saltstone-Stewart
North Bay, Ontario

Doug & Eileen Menzies
School House Antiques
Havelock, Ontario

Peter Griffiths
The Store Antiques
Toronto, Ontario

Bruce Sutton
Havelock, Ontario

Doug McCron
The Telephone Man
West Hill, Ontario

We would like to thank the following for giving so much of their time and sharing their knowledge of special categories of antiques and collectables: Jean and Lawrence Hartnell, Edith Hacking, Jack Marsden, Karen and Al Boswell, Richard Crawford, John Dunbar and Bruce Sutton.

MAGAZINES & PERIODICALS USED AS REFERENCE

Antique Showcase, Bala, Ontario
Upper Canadian, Kingston, Ontario

BISCUIT BARRELS
and
COOKIE JARS

Popular since the 1860's and still a favourite with collectors the biscuit barrel or cookie jar can be found in a variety of styles with many decorative motifs. Manufactured in Great Britain, Europe and North America the biscuit barrel was made using various materials, such as pottery, porcelain, glass, wood or metal.

CROWN MILANO GLASS BODY.
Silver plated mounts and
lid. $425.00

CRANBERRY GLASS BODY.
Silver plated mounts and
lid. $595.00

CRANBERRY GLASS BODY.
Mounts and lid require
replating. $330.00

CRANBERRY GLASS BODY.
Silver plated mounts and
lid. $295.00

CRANBERRY GLASS. Silver
plated lid. Ht. 7" . . $325.00

CRANBERRY GLASS.
Clear finial. Ht. 7½" $365.00

WEDGWOOD BODY. White on green, silver plated mounts and lid. $500.00

COBALT BLUE GLASS INSERT. Silver plated frame and lid. $325.00

BRISTOL GLASS BODY. Hand painted floral decoration, silver plated mounts and lid. $295.00

BRISTOL GLASS BODY. Hand painted daisies, mounts and lid require replating. $160.00

CHINA BODY. Silver plated
mounts and lid. $150.00

CHINA BODY. Silver plated
mounts and lid. $140.00

CHINA BODY. Silver plated
mounts and lid. $130.00

SHELLEY CHINA BODY. Silver
plated mounts and lid. $135.00

Above — Left —
WORCESTER CHINA BODY.
Silver plated mounts and
lid. $460.00
Above — Right —
CHINA BODY. Silver plated
mounts and lid. . . 165.00

CHINA BODY. Silver
plated mounts and
lid. $150.00

POTTERY. Decorated in the
oriental style. $85.00

WOOD BODY, porcelain lined,
nickel plated mounts and
lid. $145.00

COOKIE JARS — Left to Right —
Cinderella. By Napco, Japan, 1957. Ht. 9½" . . . . $ 60.00
Red Riding Hood. By Napco, Japan. Ht. 9½" 60.00
Snow White. Seven dwarfs round skirt. Disney copyright,
made in Japan, maker not known. Light weight. Ht. 9½"
Rare. 125.00

COOKIE JAR. Hey Diddle-Diddle.
1950's. Yellow ground, pink lips and
cheeks, blue and brown trim.
Ht. 10" $100.00

COOKIE JAR. Pontiac Indian. By
McCoy Pottery Co., Roseville, Ohio.
1954 - 56. Comes in light and dark
glaze. Ht. 11" $200.00

NOTE: Made as a promotional item for
the Pontiac car, but never used for that
purpose.

COOKIE JAR. Jukebox Remote Control. Imported by Vancor, Salt Lake City, Utah, 1980's. Chrome colour with red letters and numerals.
Ht. 10" $125.00

NOTE; Names of tunes/performers are related to snacks — e.g. Elvis Pretzel.

COOKIE JAR. Paddle Wheel Tug Boat. By American Bisque, Williamstown, W.Va., 1950's. Brown and green with blue paddle wheel. Bell inside lid helps prevent theft of cookies.
Ht. 9" L. 10½" $85.00

COOKIE JAR. Yellow apple with rosy cheeks, green leaf handle. McCoy Pottery Co., Roseville, Ohio, 1950 - 54.
Ht. 7" $40.00

NOTE: Similar jars made by other companies.

COOKIE JAR. Coffee Mill. By McCoy Pottery Co., Roseville, Ohio, 1961 - 68. Wood graining under glaze, "Cookies" in red, black handle and knob. $40.00

COOKIE JAR. Basketweave base, lamb's head lid. Brown with yellow bow, lamb has leaf in mouth. Late 1950's. Ht. 10" $45.00

NOTE: This base available with other lids.

COOKIE JAR. Pig, by Shawnee Pottery Co., Zanesville, Ohio. Underglaze paint, green shamrocks and trim on cream ground. Pronounced eyelashes are a feature of the Shawnee pottery. Ht. 11" $90.00

COOKIE JAR. Duncan Hines promotional jar. 1960's. Canada marked on base, maker not known. Brown bear holding cookie wearing pink sweater. Ht. 11" $90.00

COOKIE JAR. Cowboy Boots. By American Bisque, Williamstown, W.Va. Glazed pottery, brown and buff with "Cowboy Boot Cookies" on the front. Unique design, only jar in the shape of boots. Ht. 12" .. $150.00

BLACK COLLECTABLES

COOKIE JARS. By the National Silver Co. Both cold painted.
Left — Chef. Blue striped apron and buttons, dark cream ground.
Ht. 10½" $150.00
Right — Mammy. Blue trimmed apron with green dots, blue hair
ribbon, dark cream ground. Ht. 10" 150.00

COOKIE JAR. By Canuck Pottery, St.
John, N.B. 1950 - 60 (now out of business). Red clay, painted under glaze.
Dark brown lid. Body — browns and
yellows on blue and white ground.
Ht. 10" $175.00
NOTE: Similar jars came with assorted scenes.

COOKIE JAR. World Globe With Airplane. By McCoy Pottery Co., Roseville, Ohio. 1960 only. Cold painted
gold base, blue ground is glazed. Continent of Africa painted black, some
paint flaking, but most remaining.
Ht. 10" $175.00

COOKIE JAR. "The Cauliflower Mammy" By McCoy Pottery Co., Roseville, Ohio, 1939. Green, yellow, blue and brown on cream ground.
Ht. 11" $300.00

NOTE: This cookie jar, the first one made by McCoy, was coloured using the cold painted process, although paint has worn off, it is the best example of this type seen.

COOKIE JAR. By McCoy Pottery Co., Roseville, Ohio. 1948 - 57. Red, brown and green on cream ground. $150.00

NOTE: McCoy only made two of this type of cookie jar, this is the second.

COLD PAINTED: Not fired and not glazed, paint wears off with use.

COOKIE JAR. "Plain Apron Mammy" Made in Japan. Red and blue apron, red bandana. 1950's. Ht. 10"
Cold painted $150.00

COOKIE JAR. Made in Japan, marked "Sears Roebuck" on base. 1978.
Ht. 10" $200.00

SALT & PEPPER SETS.
Left — Chef & Mammy. With gold spoons. Made in Japan.
Chef 4½" tall. . . . . Pair $50.00
Right — Chef & Cook. Made in Occupied Japan.
Ht. 3½" . . . . Pair   50.00

SALT & PEPPER SETS.
Left — With watermelon. Blue and red striped suits. Pair . . $35.00
Right — Chef & Maid. Ht. 2¾" . . . . Pair   35.00

SALT & PEPPER SETS.
Left — Cook & Chef. White and black ground with red
and blue. Unmarked. Ht. 4½" Rare. . . . . Pair $40.00
Right — Valentine Couple. Marked "Shafford" Ca. 1950.
Multi-coloured, boy holding red heart. Ht. 4½" . . Pair   60.00

15

"HUGGIES" Salt & Pepper. Design by Van Tellingen. Made by Regal China. Ht. 3½" $65.00

SALT & PEPPER. Made in Japan, 1960's. Chef 4" tall. $35.00

NOTE: Came with assorted coloured hats and spoons and in various sizes.

Plastic by F. & F. Moulding Works, Dayton, Ohio. 1940's. Red, yellow and black. Premium from Quaker Oats.

UNCLE MOSE & AUNT JEMIMA SALT & PEPPER. Pair . . $25.00
AUNT JEMIMA SYRUP. Ht. 6" 55.00

Left —
CHEF & MAMMY.
Made in Japan, 1960's. With spoons, red and yellow trim. Mammy's apron marked "Wasaga Beach, Canada" Chef 5½" tall.
Pair $40.00

16

PLANTERS —
Left — Girl and corn cob. Made in Japan, 1950's. Ht. 5" . . $40.00
Centre — Boy with palm tree. Made in Japan, 1950's. Ht. 4" 40.00
Right — Boy with watermelon. Made in Occupied Japan.
1945 - 52. Ht. 4½" 40.00

ASH TRAYS —
Left — Made in Japan. 1950's. Length 4½" $45.00
Right — Baby on bed pan. "Sarnia" on one side "for old
butts and ashes" on the other. 30.00

Left —
"JUNGLE JUICE" BOTTLE.
1950's.
Ht. 7½" $50.00
Right —
CLOWN DECANTER.
Carrying four shot mugs.
1960's. 65.00

FIVE PIECE BAND. Marked "Occupied Japan" 1945 - 52.
Height of tallest 5"
Complete set $150.00

Left —
HEUBACH BISQUE.
"Dark Secret"
1900 - 1920's.
Rare.
Ht. 6½" $200.00
Right —
GERMAN BISQUE.
Children on chamber
pot. Ca. 1910.
Ht. 4" 125.00

Right —
HUMIDOR. Bisque boy's head.
German, not marked, Ca. 1870 -
1890. Green and red head-dress.
Ht. 5" $600.00

HEAD VASES. Two on right made in Japan, 1950's - 60's.
Tallest 6½" high.
Each $55.00 $45.00 $40.00

WALL POCKETS. Made in Japan, 1950's - 60's. The one
on right can either stand or hang. Tallest 5½" high.
Each $50.00

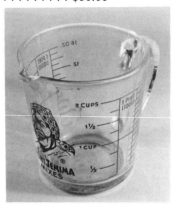

Right —
FIRE KING MEASURING CUP.
16 oz. Quaker Oats promotion,
1950's. Red Aunt Jemima.
Rare, only one seen. $65.00

19

BOTTLES

GREEN VIOLIN BOTTLES. With musical notation hang-up frame. Bottles 9½" high, frame 16" long. $90.00

VIOLIN BOTTLE. Greenish/amber, embossed with a horse head. Maker unknown. Riding crop hanger. Ht. 8½" $48.00

BANJO BOTTLE. Aquamarine. Frame, 12" long. 1950's. $45.00

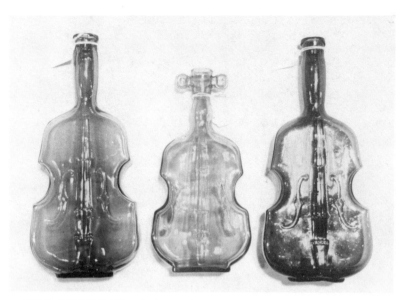

VIOLIN BOTTLES — Left to Right —
Green, by Dell Glass Co., Wheaton, N.J. Ht. 9½" $25.00
Blue, maker unknown. Ht. 8" 25.00
Amethyst, by Dell Glass Co. Ht. 9½" 34.00

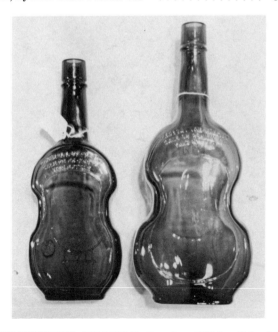

AMBER WHISKIES. "Old Fiddle Bourbon Whiskey" Bardstown
Distillery, Bardstown, Kentucky." 1950 - 60's.
Left — Ht. 9½"   . . . . $15.00   Right — Ht. 11" $15.00

VIOLIN BOTTLES. In hanger frames.
Left — Pale blue, Ht. 7½" $35.00
Centre — Pale amber, Ht. 6" 25.00
Right — Forest green, Ht. 7½" 25.00

VIOLIN VASES. In hanger frames. By Dell Glass Co.
Left — Amber, Ht. 7½" $25.00
Right — Cranberry, Ht. 7½" 85.00

JAMES B. BEAM DISTILLING CO., Clermont, Kentucky.

The first Jim Beam Regal china decanter was issued in 1953. Made to contain Kentucky Straight Bourbon.

From:
The Canadian Game Fish Series.

Above — Left —
JIM BEAM: BASS.
1973 . . . . $40.00 - $50.00
Above — Right —
JIM BEAM: RAINBOW TROUT.
1975 . . . . 50.00 - 60.00
Right —
JIM BEAM: SPECKLED TROUT.
1975/76   40.00 - 50.00

Two of the four Champion Dog Series after the paintings of James Lockhart.
Left —
JIM BEAM: SPRINGER SPANIEL.
1970. . . . . $35.00
Right —
JIM BEAM: LABRADOR RETRIEVER. 1970. . . 35.00

JIM BEAM: FIRE TRUCK.
1980/81. . . . . . . $125.00 - $140.00

JIM BEAM: SCREAMING
EAGLES. 1977.
A tribute to the 101st
Airborne Division. $85.00

JIM BEAM: SATURDAY
EVENING POST.
1975. . . . . . . $60.00

JIM BEAM: THE ANTIQUE
TRADER. 1968. . . $65.00

Stone Ginger Beers

Gurd's, Montreal, Que. . . . . Each $45.00

O'Keefe's Advertising Sign.
Amber, black and yellow.
Ca. 1940's. $85.00

O'Keefe's
Each $65.00

Milloy, Montreal, Que.
Left $105.00
Centre 90.00
Right 105.00

Fortier, Quebec, Que.
Left $90.00
Right 70.00

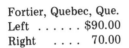

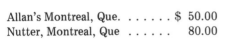

Allan's Montreal, Que. ...... $ 50.00
Nutter, Montreal, Que 80.00

Christin & Cie, Montreal, Que. $ 85.00
Christin & Cie, Montreal, Que. 100.00

26

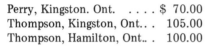

Perry, Kingston. Ont.   . . . . $ 70.00
Thompson, Kingston, Ont.. .   105.00
Thompson, Hamilton, Ont.. .   100.00

Pilgrim Bros.,
Hamilton, Ont.   . . $85.00
Cummer & Co.,
Hamilton, Ont.   . . 65.00

McLaughlin,
Toronto, Ont. . . . . $ 85.00
McLaughlin, Toronto,
Edmonton, Ottawa   165.00

Drolet & Co.,
Ottawa, Ont. $155.00
Charles Wilson,
Toronto, Ont. 145.00

Atlantic, Halifax, N.S. . . . . $ 65.00
Indian Beer, Halifax, N.S. 100.00
Dixon, Halifax, N.S. 55.00

Quinn, Halifax, N.S.
Left $65.00
Right 70.00

Roue, Halifax, N.S. . . . . $ 80.00
Roue, Halifax, N.S. 100.00
Roue, Halifax, N.S. 105.00
Roue, Halifax, N.S. 55.00

Terris, St. John, N.B.
Left . . . . $ 80.00
Centre 135.00
Right 80.00

Old Homestead, St. Stephen,
N.B. & Calais, Maine.
Left $50.00
Right 80.00

Dolan Bros., St. John, N.B. $ 75.00   Simmons, Charlottetown $225.00
Sussex Mineral Spring Co.,   120.00   Bennett, St. John's, Nfld.   135.00

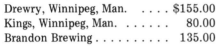

Drewry, Winnipeg, Man. $155.00
Kings, Winnipeg, Man. 80.00
Brandon Brewing 135.00

Empire Brewing, Brandon,
Man.
Left $130.00
Right 150.00

Saskatoon Bottling Works $145.00
Empire Brewing, Brandon, Man. 165.00

Kings, Winnipeg &
Saskatoon . . . . $ 80.00
Crystal Spring, Moose Jaw,
Sask. 135.00

JUG. "Victoria, Queen & Empress"
Biscuit/Brown. Ht. 7½" $350.00

JUG. "Victoria, Queen & Empress
Beige/Brown. Ht. 7½" . . $280.0

Phillips, Calgary, Alberta
Left $100.00
Right 90.00

Thorpes, Vancouver, B.C.
Left . . . . $ 80.00
Right 105.00

Kirk & Co., Victoria, B.C. . . . . $ 70.00
Old English Beverage Co., Victoria, B.C.   135.00
Regal, Victoria, B.C. 65.00

Country Club
Beverage Co.
Ltd. $80.00

PERFUME BOTTLES.

Left to Right —
French Opaline, white with
gold trim. Ca. 1900.
Ht. 9" . . . . $ 95.00
R.S. Germany porcelain.
Roses on yellow and white
ground, gold stopper.
Ca. 1900. Ht. 4" . . 125.00
French Bristol type. Gold,
blue and green geometric
design. Ca. 1870. . . 145.00

JUG. "Victoria, Queen & Empress"
Biscuit/Brown. Ht. 6¾" $350.00

PERFUME BOTTLES.

Left to Right —
Bristol glass, turquoise
blue. Ca. 1890's.
Ht. 6½" . . . . $ 85.00
Bohemian glass, black
with floral and gold
decoration.
Ca. 1870. . . 125.00
French opaline, green.
Ca. 1890's. Stopper
not original. 65.00

**VASELINE GLASS
PERFUME BOTTLES.**
Left to Right —

Baccarat Swirl pattern.
Ht. 6½" . . . . $150.
Block pattern.
Ht. 5½" . . . . 95.
Diagonal Block
pattern. Ht. 6½" . . 145.

JUG. "Victoria, Queen & Empress"
Pale green and white on royal blue
ground, brown handle, sterling rim.
Ht. 7½" $425.00

"FOR THE QUEEN'S JUBILEE 1837 - 1887"
Part of a tea service commemorating Queen
Victoria's Golden Jubilee. Brown on white
ground. Teapot 9" high. Sugar 7" high.
Teapot, sugar, cup & saucer. $1000.00

Mark on tea service.
R.H. Plant & Co.
Longton, Staffordshire,
England.

Above — Left —
PLATE. 1837 - 1887. Queen Victoria's
Golden Jubilee. Black on white ground,
blue trim. Diam. 10¼" . . . . $ 85.00
Above — Right —
PLATE. 1837 - 1897. Queen Victoria's
Diamond Jubilee. Diam. 9½"   150.00
Left —
PLATE. "Victoria Diamond Jubilee
1897. Longest Reign on Record."
Empress of India
Queen of England
Crowned 1837"
Diam. 9½" 155.00

STAFFORDSHIRE MUGS. Commemorating Queen Victoria's Diamond
Jubilee, 1897. Left — Purple on white. Ht. 3¼" $60.00
Right — Purple and blue on white. 85.00

Above — Left & Right —
BEAKER. Commemorating Queen
Victoria's Diamond Jubilee, 1897.
Brown on off white ground.
Marked Doulton, Burslem.
Ht. 4" $125.00

Left —
BEAKER. Commemorating Queen
Victoria's Diamond Jubilee, 1897.
Enamelware.
Ht. 4" 85.00

KING EDWARD VII (1841 - 1910)
Accession   January 22, 1901
Coronation   August 9, 1902

Mark on plate at left.
Britannia Porcelan Works,
Karlsbad, Austria.

EDWARD VII
"God bless our King.
In commemoration of the
accession to the throne of
his R.H. the Prince of Wales
22 January, 1901."
Gold edged plate with black
and white portrait.
Diam. 8½" $65.00

PLATE. Commemorating the
coronation of Edward VII and
Queen Alexander.Cream ground
with portraits and blue and gold
trim. Marked Royal Doulton.
Diam. 9"
Mint condition. $140.00

CHILD'S ALPHABET PLATE. Tin,
embossed "The Prince & Princess of
Wales" with two heads. Believed to
be Edward and Alexander.
Late 1800's. Diam. 6" $35.00

POST CARD. Black and white.
Queen Alexander and King Edward.
Postmarked Oct. 6. 1906. . . $15.00

37

ENAMELWARE BEAKER.
Edward VII & Queen Alexander.
Ht. 3¾" $50.00

ROYAL DOULTON BEAKER.
Edward VII & Queen Alexander.
"June 1902" On reverse —
"ER, King's Coronation Dinner,
Presented by His Majesty."
Green on white ground.
Ht. 4" $65.00

LITHOPHANE MUG. Commemorating
the Coronation of Edward VII, 1902.
Ht. 2¾" $125.00

Lithophane illustration of
Edward VII in base of mug
at left.

LITHOPHANE: A decorative transparency of transluscent porcelain. The
illustration becomes visible when viewed by transmitted light.

DEMI-TASSE. Coronation commemorative. Edward VII and Queen Alexander. On reverse of cup "Coronation of King Edward the VII. June 26th 1902." White ground with full colour portraits and gold trim. Cup 2¼" high. $95.00

DEMI-TASSE. Cream ground, full colour portraits, gold trim. On cups "H.M. King Edward VII" and "H.M. Queen Alexander." On saucers "God Save The King" Cups 2¼" high. . . . . Pair $75.00

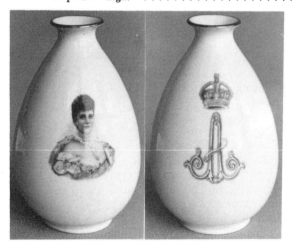

Left —
ROYAL DOULTON VASE. Commemorating Queen Alexander's visit to the Doulton factory.
Ht. 3½" $75.00

KING GEORGE V (1865 - 1936)
Accession   May 6, 1910
Coronation   June 22, 1911

Right —
"H.M. KING GEORGE V"
Plaque with portrait on white ground,
gold trim and open work.
Diam. 5" $35.00

PLATE. Coronation commemorative.
"Peace & Happiness, King George V
& Queen Mary, crowned June 22, 1911,
Long May They Reign." White ground,
gold trim. Marked Grimwades Royal
Winton Faience. Diam. 9½"
Hairline crack. $125.00

PLATE. "H.M. Queen Mary,
H.M. King George V"
"Silver Jubilee 1910 - 1935"
By James Kent Ltd., England.
Diam. 10¾" $55.00

TEAPOT. Commemorating Silver Jubilee. "Queen Mary, King George,
1910 - 1935" Marked Maling Ware, Ringtons Ltd., Newcastle-on-Tyne"
Ht. 4¾" $135.00

Left —
TOOTHPICK HOLDERS.
Portraits of King George V
and Queen Mary on white
ground.
Ht. 2"
Pair $65.00

COMMEMORATIVE BEAKERS. King George V & Queen Mary.
Left — "Long May They Reign" Coronation, 1911. Ht. 4¼" $75.00
Right — "Silver Jubilee 1910 - 1935" Ht. 4½" 55.00

COMMEMORATIVE MUGS. King George V & Queen Mary. Left to Right —
Coronation, 1911. By Jackson & Gosling Grovenor China, England.
Ht. 3¼" $35.00
"Dieu et mon droit" (God and my Right) Austrian. 25.00
Silver Jubilee, 1935. Made in England. 35.00

41

ROYAL DOULTON MUGS. Queen Mary and King George V. On reverse "Peace & Victory 1919" White ground decorated with brown portraits, garlands and lettering. Ht. 3" . . . . Pair $150.00

Left —
ROYAL DOULTON CREAM JUG.
Coronation commemorative,
King George V.
Ht. 3" $65.00

TIN. Featuring King George V and Queen Mary, Edward The Prince of Wales and Princess Mary. Crown on lid. Ca. 1914.
3½" x 4" x 4½" $70.00

TIN. King George V and Queen Mary, Princess Elizabeth & Margaret. Royal coats of arms along with events and achievements of the era are depicted. 1930's. Ht. 4½" $65.00

KING EDWARD VIII (1894 - 1972)
Accession   January 20, 1936
Abdicated   December 11, 1936

CORONATION COMMEMORATIVE.
"Coronation ER (Edward Rex)
May 12, 1937" Gold trim, oak leaves
on cream ground. Paragon China.
Diam. 4" $55.00

PLATE. "Coronation of King Edward
VIII, 12th May 1937, Long May He
Reign" White ground, blue and
orange trim.
Diam. 9" $145.00

Left —
"H.M. KING EDWARD VIII
CORONATION 1937"
White silhouette on blue
ground.
Diam. 5½" $40.00

MUG. "King Edward VIII Crowned
12th May 1937"
Ht. 3" $65.00

MUG. "Coronation May 12th 1937,
H.M. Edward VIII"
Ht. 4" $65.00

43

KING GEORGE VI (1895 - 1952)
Accession   December 11, 1936
Coronation   May 12, 1937

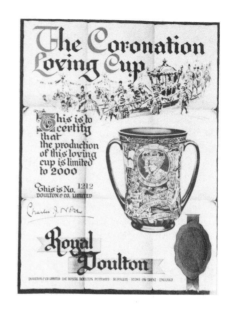

Right —
THE CORONATION LOVING
CUP.
Certificate of Limited Edition.
1212/2000.

Above — Left & Right —
THE CORONATION LOVING CUP.
By Royal Doulton.
King George VI & Queen Elizabeth,
May, 1937.
Limited edition No. 1212/2000.
Ht. 10¼" $1200.00

Left—
Base of Coronation Loving Cup.

44

SOVEREIGN POTTERS
CANADA
K.

Mark on plate below.

PLATE. "Coronation George VI,
Elizabeth May 12th 1937"
With a portrait of Princess Eliz-
abeth. Diam. 6" $45.00

PLATE.
"Coronation H.M. King George VI &
Queen Elizabeth, 12th May 1937"
Marked Sovereign Potters, Canada.
Diam. 10½" $35.00

Mark on plate at left.

Above —
PLATE. "King George VI & Queen
Elizabeth Royal Visit to Canada
May, 1939" Cream ground, gold
trim. Marked Sovereign, Canada.
Diam. 9" $65.00
Right —
PLATE. "Long May They Reign.
Commemorating Royal visit to
Canada and U.S.A., 1939. Cream
ground, gold trim. Johnson Bros.,
England. Diam. 10" 45.00

45

PLATES. "Long May They Reign. To commemorate the visit of their Majesties King George VI and Queen Elizabeth to Canada and the United States of America, May, 1939."

Left   — Cream ground, gold trim. Nelson Ware, England. $25.00
Right   — Off white ground, gold and blue trim.
             Wellington China, England. 30.00

Above — Left —
PLATE. "King George VI, Queen Elizabeth Royal Visit to Canada, May, 1939" Marked Sovereign, Canada, British Empire Made. Diam. 7½" $65.00
Above — Right —
PLATE. "1939 Royal Visit to Canada, King George VI & Queen Elizabeth" Cream ground, gold trim with medallions depicting Princess Elizabeth & Princess Margaret. Alfred Meakin, England. Diam. 8¼" 55.00

Left —
PLATE. "Commemorating The Visit Of Their Majesties To The United States Of America, 1939, King George VI & Queen Elizabeth" Pink on cream ground. Marked Royal Ivory, John Maddock & Son, England. 9" x 9" 55.00

46

COMMEMORATIVE MUG.
Coronation, 1937.
"George VI & Queen Eliz-
abeth. Ht. 3½"   . . $40.00

CHARACTER JUG. By Royal
Winton, Grimwades, England.
George VI in naval uniform.
Ht. 4" $50.00

CORONATION COMMEMORATIVE. May, 1937.
King George VI. Silver plated tea strainer with china
base. L. 4½" $65.00

NOT SHOWN —

CAKE PLATE. China with nickel plated centre handle. Commemorating
the Coronation of George Vi, May, 1937 with Canadian crest.
7¾" square. $55.00
CUP & SAUCER. "King George Vi & Queen Elizabeth. Royal Visit to
Canada, May, 1939" 35.00
PITCHER. Marked "Medalta" Commemorating Coronation of George
VI & Queen Elizabeth, May 12, 1937.
"Dieu et mon Droit" (God and my right) 45.00

47

QUEEN ELIZABETH II (1926 -)

Accession February 6, 1952   Coronation June 2, 1953

THE CORONATION LOVING CUP.
By Royal Doulton.
On reverse — Elizabeth I.
Limited edition No. 845/1000.
Ht. 10½" $1200.00

CORONATION LOVING CUP.
Certificate of limited edition.

COMMEMORATIVE MUGS. Obverse and reverse.
"H.M. Queen Elizabeth II, Crowned 2nd June 1953" Gold Queen's
Beast handle and trim. Bone china by Arthur Bowker, Staffordshire.
Ht. 2½" . . . . Each . . $50.00

QUEEN'S BEASTS: Ten statues of Heraldic creatures which were sculpted to
stand guard outside the Annexe, Westminster Abbey, where Queen Elizabeth II
arrived for her Coronation.

48

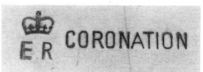

Left —
OAK STOOL. Black velvet seat with gold braid trim.
Provided for the invited guests at Westminster Abbey Coronation ceremony, Elizabeth II, June 2, 1953.
19" x 18" x 12½" $250.00

Above — Left —
PLATE. "June 2, 1953 Coronation, Elizabeth II" Blue decoration and Royal insignia. Burleigh Ware, England. Diam. 9¾" $65.00
Above — Right —
PLATE. "The Coronation of Her Majesty Queen Elizabeth, June 2nd 1953" Marked Sovereign Potters, Made in Canada.
Diam. 8" 40.00
Left —
PLATE. "H.M. Queen Elizabeth II June 2nd 1953 Coronation.
White ground, gold trim, decorated with thistles, shamrocks and roses. Tuscan Bone China, England.
Diam. 8" 70.00

COMMEMORATIVE JUG.
"June 2, 1953, Coronation
Elizabeth II"
Ht. 3½" $35.00

COMMEMORATIVE MUG.
"ER II, Coronation, June 2,
1953" Marked Royal Albert
Bone China, England.
Ht. 3" $45.00

CUP & SAUCER. Commemorating
the opening of the St. Lawrence
Seaway by Queen Elizabeth and
President Eisenhower.
1959.   . . . . $85.00

Right —
BOWL. "To Commemorate The
Queen's Silver Jubilee"
"1952 - 1977"
Brown on biscuit pottery.
Diam. 7" $35.00

QUEEN ELIZABETH II SILVER JUBILEE COMMEMORATIVE MUGS.
Tallest mug 4¾" high. Values . . . . $15.00   to $45.00

COVERED VASE. To commemorate
the Silver Jubilee of Queen Elizabeth.
Hand painted with Buckingham Palace
on obverse, dates of British monarchs
on reverse. By Aynsley, England,
signed L. Woodhouse. Limited edition
of 100. Ht. 14" $4500.00

WEDGWOOD PLATE.
White on blue. "Silver Jubilee,
Queen Elizabeth II, 1952 -
1977"
Diam. 8" $55.00
Not Shown —
WEDGWOOD PLAQUE.
Blue on cream. "Coronation
Jubilee, H.M. Queen Eliza-
beth II, 1953 - 1978"
Diam. 8" 50.00

51

QUEEN ELIZABETH, THE QUEEN MOTHER.
80th BIRTHDAY, August 4th 1980.
Left — Crown Staffordshire Coaster.
Diam. 4" $15.00
Right — Mug. President of the National
Trust. Made by Boncath Pottery.
Ht. 3½" 10.00

Left —
PORTRAIT PLATE.
On back "Her Majesty Queen Elizabeth,
The Queen Mother, 85th Birthday
Celebration" (1985). By Rosina China
Co. Ltd, England. Diam. 8" $175.00

Mark on portrait plate at left.

Left —
PORTRAIT PLATE. Prince Philip.
White ground, gold trim. From the
Royal Family Series. Made in England,
decorated in Canada.
Diam. 8" . . . . $ 95.00

52

WEDGWOOD PLATES. Diced, white, lilac and sage green. Diam. 9"
Left — "H.R.H. The Prince of Wales, Royal Wedding, 1981"
     No. 18/250. .... $2750.00
Right — "H.R.H. The Princess of Wales, Royal Wedding, 1981"
     No. 72/250. .... 2750.00

WEDGWOOD PLATES. Commemorating the Royal Wedding,
July 29, 1981. White on blue.
Left — Diam. 8" .... $ 50.00
Right — Diam. 6½" 40.00

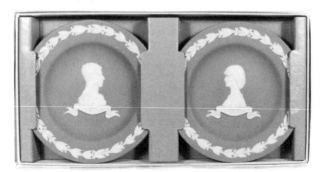

WEDGWOOD ROYAL WEDDING COMMEMORATIVES.
White on blue. Boxed .... $ 40.00

Left —
ROYAL WEDDING
COMMEMORATIVE.
The Prince and Princess of Wales,
July 29, 1981.
Coalport bone china modelled
by John Bromley.
No. 89/500.
Ht. 8" L. 10" $2000.00

Above —
PLATE. "H.R.H. The Prince of Wales
and Lady Diana Spencer, 29th July 1981.
To commemorate their marriage in St.
Paul's Cathedral" Black on white ground.
Enoch Wood, Tunstall, England.
Diam. 10" $45.00

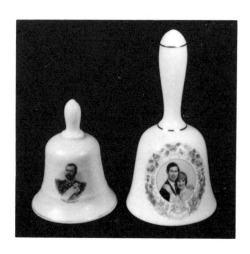

Above —
PORTRAIT THIMBLE.
Commemorating the betrothel
announcement, Prince Charles
and Lady Diana. Feb. 24, 1981.
Thimble 1" high.   . . $15.00

BELLS.
Left — Portrait of King George
V on cream ground.
Ht. 3½" $35.00
Right — Birth of Prince William,
June 21, 1982. White ground,
gold trim.
Crown Staffordshire.   25.00

54

CANADIAN SOUVENIR.
Glass paperweight. Queen
Victoria, beaver and
date 1837. . . . . $75.00

ETCHED GLASS.
"1837 - 1897, Souvenir
Reinhardt & Co., Toronto"
Ht. 3½" $35.00

Left —
PRESSED GLASS PLATE. Lacy
pattern by the Sandwich Glass Co.
Probably made for the Coronation
of Queen Victoria, 1837.
Inscribed "Victoria" with a border
of thistles, roses and shamrocks.
Diam. 5" $125.00

Right —
PRESSED GLASS PLATE.
Commemorating Queen Victoria's
Golden Jubilee. Diam. 10¼" $125.00

PRESSED GLASS BISCUIT JAR.
"1910 - 1935 To Commemorate
The 25th Year of Their Reign."
George V & Queen Mary.
Ht. 9¾" Mint $140.00

PRESSED GLASS HALF-PINT
TANKARD. "May 6th 1935
Silver Jubilee"
George V & Queen Mary.
Ht. 4¼" $95.00

PRESSED GLASS HALF-PINT
TANKARD. "Long Live The
King Crowned May, 1937"
"King George VI & Queen
Elizabeth"
Ht. 4¼" $85.00

PRESSED GLASS DISH. "Coronation of
H.M. King George VI, 1937"
Diam. 7¼" $65.00

WEBB CORBETT GLASS LOVING
CUP. Coronation commemorative.
"ER II, 1953"
Ht. 5" $175.00

WEDGWOOD GOBLET. Amethyst &
clear. Jasper cameo of Queen Elizabeth II. Silver Jubilee, 1977.
No. 160/500. Ht. 5¼" $200.00

GOBLETS. Webb Corbett hand cut lead crystal.
Left — Queen Elizabeth, The Queen Mother, 80th birthday, Aug. 4, 1980.
No. 212/1000. Ht. 8¾" $500.00
Right— Wedding of Prince Charles and Lady Diana, July 29, 1981.
No. 86/1000. Ht. 8½" 500.00

Right —
CIGARETTE BOX. Brass.
A gift to the troops in France,
Christmas, 1914 from Princess
Mary, The Princess Royal, only
daughter of George V and Queen
Mary. Contained specially mono-
grammed cigarettes.
1" x 3¼" x 5" $100.00

Left —
GILDED LOCKET/BOOK.
With photos of Queen Victoria,
Edward VII and Alexander,
George V & Mary and
Edward, Prince of Wales.
Early 1900's.
Closed 1" x 1½" $55.00

Left —   WATCH FOB. Celluloid. Independent
Order of Foresters. Queen Victoria's Diamond
Jubilee, 1897. . . . . $45.00
Right — PIN BACK BUTTON. Litho-tin.
"An Empire Mourns, 1819 - 1901"   25.00

MEDALLION. Gilded brass
with crown pin. Made to
commemorate   Queen
Victoria's Diamond Jubilee,
1897.
In photo — Queen Victoria,
Prince Edward, Prince George
and Edward Prince of Wales.
Length 3¼" $100.00

Left — PIN BACK BUTTON. Litho-tin.
George V & Queen Elizabeth. $18.00
Right — PIN BACK BUTTON. Celluloid.
"The Canadian Century, Montreal, Canada"
George V & Queen Mary. 15.00

58

Above — Left —
BROOCH. Silver colour with crown
pin. Commemorating Queen Victoria's
Diamond Jubilee, 1897.   . . . . $15.00
Above — Right —
BROOCH. Gold colour with red,
white and blue ribbon. George VI &
Queen Elizabeth.
Dated 1939.   . . . .   20.00
Below — Left —
BUTTON. Silverplated copper.
"Elizabeth The Second" 15.00
Below — Right —
ENAMEL PIN. Blue and white.
Elizabeth II, Silver Jubilee 15.00

PUZZLES.
Left — Waddington's.
"Queen Victoria's State
Bedroom, Woburn Abbey"
Complete. . . . . $ 65.00
Right — Chad Valley Toys.
Edward VII.
Complete. 125.00

Left —
PIN BACK BUTTON. Full colour litho-tin.
Royal Wedding, July 29, 1981.
Diam. 2¼" $5.00

CERAMICS

CHEESE DISH. Jackfield Pottery, Shropshire, England. Multi-coloured decoration on black ground. Diam. 12½" $325.00

CHEESE DISH. Adams, white on sage green ground. Diam. 10" $350.00

Left —
CHEESE DISH. Floral decoration on white ground. Diam. 8" $100.00

Right —
CHEESE DISH. Cottage shape, brown roof. Ht. 5" $40.00

Above — Left —
WEDGE SHAPE CHEESE
DISH. Floral decoration
on white ground, twig
and acorn handle.
Ht. 6" $75.00
Above — Right —
WEDGE SHAPE CHEESE
DISH. Floral decoration
on cream ground.   55.00
Left —
SLAB SHAPE CHEESE
DISH. Pink and mauve
on white ground.   60.00

Right —
SLAB SHAPE CHEESE
DISH. Richly decorated
in rust shades on cream
ground. $90.00

Left —
SLAB SHAPE CHEESE
DISH. Delicate floral
decoration on cream
ground. $30.00

LIDDED JUG. Stoneware with a salt glaze, moulded floral pattern. Ca. 1850. Ht. 9½" . . $125.00

JUG. Stoneware with a salt glaze, moulded pattern of birds and foliage. $135.00

JUG. Copper lustre with moulded pattern of Pirouette and Columbine. Early 19th century. Ht. 8" $150.00

JUG. Copper lustre with decorative deep blue band round top, purple lustre floral decoration on white band. Ht. 5¼" $85.00

TEAPOT. Sunderland lustre. Early 1800's. L. 12" $295.00

TEAPOT & PLATE. Liverpool pottery, Ca. 1830. Transfer
decoration. $225.00

BELLEEK BAMBOO TEAPOT. White, blue and pink. Ht. 5"
Marked with second black mark (1891 - 1926) $700.00

TEAPOT. Sunderland lustre. Early 1800's. Pink on cream
ground. Ht. 8" $325.00

TEAPOT. Jackfield Pottery. Multi-coloured decoration on
black ground. Ht. 5½" $165.00

Left —
TEAPOT. Copper lustre,
floral decoration. $200.00

Ornaments and Figures

GAMEBIRD. Good detail, bright colours. Ht. 9" $125.00

COCKATOOS. Bright-coloured with high crest. Ht 7" $110.00

CARDINAL. Marked "Stangl Pottery Birds" (Trenton, N.J.) Ca. 1941. One of the Stangl Audubon series. Red and black, blue/green & yellow stump. Ht. 7" $90.00

PARROT. Orange, olive green and blue. Ht. 9" .. $145.00

COPELAND PARIAN.
"Go To Sleep" Designed by
I. Durham, Art Union of
London, 1862.   . . $2000.00

ROYAL DUX COUPLE. Shades
of muted browns and greens.
Ca. 1923. Ht. 18"
Pair $850.00

NOT SHOWN —

BISQUE. German nodders, lady
and gentleman in period dress.
Ca. 1890. Pair $275.00

STAFFORDSHIRE. Cottage
shape pastille burner.
Ca. 1840. . . . .   335.00

STAFFORDSHIRE. Spaniels.
Pair. 565.00

STAFFORDSHIRE. Spill vase,
tiger and stag.
Ca. 1850 - 60. . . . . . .   265.00

Left —
BRONZE HUNTER & WOLF.
Knife missing from right hand.
On marble base. Signed Etrope
Douret (1833 - 1906) Mid to
late 1800's.
Ht. 16" $2500.00

BISQUE FIGURES. "Just Like
Mama & Pappa" Decorated in
pastels and gilt. Ht. 10"
Pair $110.00

BISQUE FIGURES. Decorated
with blue and red, removeable
glasses. Tallest 5½" high. Not
old. Pair $50.00

BISQUE FIGURE CANDLE
STICK. Richly decorated.
Ht. 9" $95.00

BISQUE FIGURES. "The Snow-
ballers" Vividly decorated. Early
1900's. Ht. 9½"
Pair $150.00

NODDERS

NODDING FIGURES. Made in Japan, brightly painted pottery, 1950's.
Left to Right —
POLICEMAN,
Ht. 6" $35.00 - $45.00
FISHERMAN,
Ht. 7¼" $35.00 - $45.00
GOLFER,
Ht. 6" $35.00 - $45.00

NODDING FIGURES. Made in Japan, 1950's.
Left to Right —
SHRINER,
Ht. 7" $55.00
SCOTSMAN,
Ht. 7" 35.00
CANADIAN MOUNTIE,
Ht. 7" 25.00

NODDING FIGURES. The Beatles, made in Japan for Car Mascots Inc., Los Angeles, California. Multi-coloured composition.
Left to Right — Ringo Starr; Paul McCartney; John Lennon and George Harrison.   Set $350.00

KISSING NODDERS. Japanese, papier-mache with magnetic lips.
Left — Cowgirl and Cowboy. On base "Let's Kiss"
Pair . . . . $35.00 - $40.00
Right — Oriental Couple. On base "Let's Kiss" These nodders
are also coin banks. Lady, 5¾" high.
Pair . . . . $35.00 - $40.00

NODDING FIGURE. Mickey
Mouse, Made in the U.S.A.
Walt Disney Productions, 1960.
Ht. 7½" $25.00

NODDING FIGURE. Made in
West Germany, papier-mache.
Ht. 5½"
With original tag. $35.00

LIMOGES COFFEE SET. Hand painted flowers, pink, orange, turquoise and green with gold trim. Artist signed "RIRI" Coffee Pot 10½" high.
Set $425.00

MARK ON COFFEE SET. "Elite Works/SM/Limoges/ France"
(Guerin-Pouyat - Elite Ltd. 1896 - 1900)

NIPPON COFFEE POT. Not marked. Richly decorated with roses, moriage and jewelling, pale cream ground.
Ht. 9" $450.00

ROYAL BONN VASE. German, late 1800's. Hand painted, decorated with flowers and gold on wine coloured ground.
Ht. 8" $175.00

70

Left —
GAUDY IRONSTONE
JUG. Brightly decorated
in impressionistic style
with grape and vine.
Ht. 5" $130.00

Right —
JUG. Sunderland lustre.
Green, pink and gold.
Ht. 6" $230.00

Left —
JUG. Made in Stafford-
shire, England by Brown-
field & Son, Late 1800's.
White ground decorated
with purple.
Ht. 8" $145.00

Right —
GAUDY WELSH JUG.
With Imari-type decor-
ation — reds, blue, greens
and gold.
Ht. 7½" $175.00

IRISH BELLEEK

1891 - 1926

BELLEEK BREAD PLATE.
Shamrock pattern on basket-
weave. Diam. 6½"
Ca. 1930 . . . . . . $50.00

black: 1927 -1941
green: 1946 -1955

Left — BELLEEK LOW CUP & SAUCER. Shamrock pattern on basketweave with bamboo handle. Ca. 1901 - 25. . . . . $105.00
Right — BELLEEK TALL CUP & SAUCER. Shamrock pattern on basketweave with bamboo handle. Ca. 1930. . . . . 95.00

BELLEEK CREAM & SUGAR. Shamrock pattern on basketweave
with bamboo handles. Ca. 1930. . . . . Pair $145.00

BELLEEK SHELL PATTERN.
Left — Toy creamer, handle and base decorated with coral pink. Ht. 3"
Ca. 1901. . . $150.00
Right — Individual creamer. Ht. 3¾"
Ca. 1930. . . 75.00

BELLEEK CREAM & SUGAR. Ca. 1950.
Each $85.00

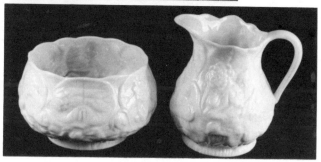

Left — BELLEEK HARP BOWL. (middle of three sizes) Ht. 1¾" L. 5"
Ca. 1901 - 25 . . $85.00

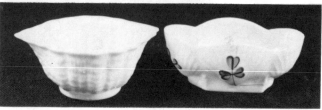

BELLEEK OPEN SALTS. Ca. 1930.
Left — Tridnaca pattern. Ht. 1¼" $65.00
Right — The Harp Shamrock. Ht. 1¼" 75.00

MOORCROFT

William Moorcroft was manager of the art pottery department of James MacIntyre & Company, Burslem, England from 1898 to 1913 when he began his own pottery, W. Moorcroft (Ltd.), Burslem. The signature mark registered as a trademark by William Moorcroft in 1919 was also used by him on articles he decorated while at the MacIntyre works. When William Moorcroft died in 1945, the pottery was taken over by his son Walter.

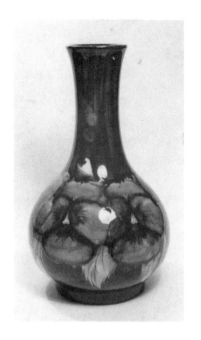

Right —
MOORCROFT VASE.
Pink and blue pansies,
yellow foliage on
cobalt blue ground.
1930's.
Ht. 12" . . $1100.00

MOORCROFT BOWL. Orchid, late 1930's. Diam. 9" $495.00
MOORCROFT VASES, late 1940's, early 1950's.
Left — 3" high, each $125.00
Right — 6" high 250.00

MOORCROFT — Left to Right —
```
VASE      ........................ $345.00
RECTANGULAR CIGARETTE BOXES. Each  ..    84.50
COVERED BOWL   ...................    325.00
VASE      ........................    320.00
OPEN BOWL ......................    265.00
```

MOORCROFT — NOT SHOWN —
Candle holder. Cobalt blue.
Ht. 6½" .... $ 55.00
Dish, leaf shape, footed. Cobalt
blue. L. 4½" 95.00
Vase. Grapes and leaves. Purple,
red and yellow. Ht. 5¾" .. 375.00
Vase. Multi-coloured flowers on
cobalt ground. Ht. 4¼" 125.00

BY APPOINTMENT.

POTTER TO
H.M.The QUEEN.

Left —
MOORCROFT
FOOTED BOWL.
Floral decoration
on cobalt blue
ground.
1960's.
Ht. 5" .. $75.00

Royal Beyreuth

ROYAL BAYREUTH. Ca. 1900. Left to Right —
VASE. Decorated with sheep. Ht. 3½"   . . . . $ 82.00
EWER. Decorated with cattle. Ht. 7½" 195.00
VASE. Decorated with cattle. Ht. 5½" 127.00

Above — ROYAL BAYREUTH. String saver decorated with fox hunting scene. Ht. 3¾" $150.00

Left — ROYAL BAYREUTH VASE. Decorated with cattle. Ht. 8½" 195.00

ROYAL BAYREUTH.
Ca. 1900.
Left —
TRIANGUALR DISH.
Rural scene. $ 95.00
Right —
DISH. "The Minstrels"
On gray ground.
4" x 4" 120.00

ROYAL BAYREUTH. Ca. 1900. Left to Right —
BON-BON DISH. Pink and yellow roses on cream ground, gold trim. $48.00
ROSE BOWL. Yellow roses, white ground. Ht. 4" 95.00
PIN TRAY. Yellow roses, cream ground, gold trim. 55.00

ROYAL BAYREUTH.
Left —
PORTRAIT BUD VASE.
Cream, blue, yellow,
cobalt blue and gold.
1890 - 1900.
Ht. 4½" $125.00
Right —
VASE. Blues, greens and
gold with peacock in
medallion.
Ht. 5¼" 250.00

Left —
ROYAL BAYREUTH
TOMATO PITCHER.
Vine handle, leaf rim and
spout. Early 1900's.
Ht. 6½" $195.00

ROYAL BAYREUTH FIGURAL PIECES. Early 1900's. Left to Right —
COVERED TOMATO DISH. Ht. 3" $57.00
SHELL. With coral handle. Ht. 4" 97.00
COVERED TOMATO DISH. Ht. 2¾" 42.00

ELK COVERED SUGAR & CREAMER. Ca. 1910 - 1915.
Sugar lid has leaf and acorn finial.
Sugar, 3" high. $300.00

ROYAL BAYREUTH CORINTHIAN PATTERN. White on
black with gold border. Left to Right —
PIN TRAY. 5" x 3½" $55.00
PLATE. Diam. 7½" 95.00
ASH TRAY. 4¼" x 4¼" 55.00

ROYAL BAYREUTH
CORINTHIAN
PATTERN.
Left — Flower Bowl.
Ht. 3½" $55.00
Right —
Creamer .. 50.00

ROYAL BAYREUTH. Left to Right —
CREAMER. "Auckland Exhibition 1913 - 1914. $110.00
TAPESTRY CREAMER. Decorated with roses
and gold trim. Ca. 1900 - 1905. Ht. 3½" 295.00
CREAMER. Roses on green ground, gold trim.
Ht. 3½" 75.00

79

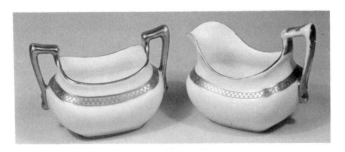

ROYAL BAYREUTH CREAMER & SUGAR. Gold geometric pattern and trim, white ground. Ht. of each 3½" Pair $47.00

ROYAL BAYREUTH TAPESTRY TRAY. Courting couple. 1890's. L. 10" $450.00

ROYAL BAYREUTH DRESSER TRAY. Roses on white ground. 1890's. 10" x 7½" $150.00

Washstand Sets

Three piece washstand or bedroom sets — large jug, wash bowl and chamber pot or sets consisting of seven or eight pieces — wash bowl, large jug, small jug (for hot water), soap dish, shaving dish, toothbrush holder, chamber pot and slop pail are becoming difficult to find.

BEDROOM SET. Grape and vine decoration on white basketweave ground. Small jug, large jug (11½" high), basin, covered soap dish, covered slop pail and covered chamber pot.   Set $600.00

BEDROOM SET. Green with gilt flowers and gold trim on white ground.
Ca. 1860. Two pieces with hairline cracks. Jug 10½" high.
Jug, basin, chamber pots, covered soap dish and sponge dish   . . $550.00

BEDROOM SET. Pink roses, gold trim on white ground. Jug 12½" high.
Jug, basin, slop pail and chamber pot $395.00

BEDROOM SET. Rudyard pattern by Samuel Ford & Co., Burslem,
England. Jug 11½" high.
Jug, basin, soap dish, toothbrush holder, pitcher and mug. $325.00

COVERED SOAP DISH AND CHAMBER POT.
English. White with beaver motif and finial.
Dish $130.00
Chamber pot 215.00

Above —
CHAMBER POT WITH
JUG & BASIN
White. Jug 12" high.
Set $125.00

Left —
JUG & BASIN.
Pink roses, gold trim on
white ground.
Jug 12" high . . 175.00

Left —
JUG & BASIN WITH
TOOTHBRUSH HOLDER.
Decorated with birds in
flight.
Jug 12" high.
Toothbrush holder 5½" high.
Set $225.00

Right —
JUG & BASIN.
Enamelware decorated with
flowers.
Jug 11½" high.   . . $95.00

Left —
JUG & BASIN.
Marked "Don, Made in
England." Band of red
roses, white ground.
Jug 10½" high. $110.00

CLOCKS

Right —
GRANDFATHER CLOCK. English, signed on dial Richard Marshall, Wolsingham. Dated 1765. 30-hour with hour strike and calendar, rope wind. Pine case, brass dial with four seasons depicted in the corners.
Ht. 79"
Width of hood 18" . . $14,000.00

Not Shown —
GRANDFATHER CLOCK. English, Sheraton style, Ca. 1770 - 90. Mahogany and walnut case inlaid with fruit woods. Painted scene depicting Daniel in the Lion's Den surrounding dial.
Ht. 95" $4500.00
GRANDFATHER CLOCK. English, Ca. 1820. 8-day, hour strike on bell. Oak case, mahogany inlay. Painted rural scene surrounding dial.
Ht. 85" 4200.00

Left —
GRANDFATHER CLOCK.
Canadian, by Twiss Bros., Montreal. 30-hour wood works. 1820's.
Pine case.
Ht. 72" $3900.00

JEROME & DARROW, Bristol, Conn. 30-hour wood works. Floral decorated wood dial, in carved case with original mirror glass. Ht. 36" W. 18" $1500.00

SETH THOMAS. 8-day, hour strike and alarm, weight driven. Dated by label 1852. Mahogany veneer case, gilded columns, original glass. Ht. 33" W. 16½" $1750.00

NEWHAVEN SHELF CLOCK. Ca. 1900. 8-day, hour strike. Ht. 17" W. 10" All original. . . $400.00

INGRAHAM. Venetian, strike on bell and alarm. Ht. 16" $450.00

TEUTONIA CLOCK CO., Baden, Germany, Ca. 1880's. 8-day, hour and ½-hour strike. Oak case, gilded dial and corners, silver chapter ring. Ht. 16" L. 12" $1200.00

SETH THOMAS. 8-day Westminster chime with strike/silent and regulator dials. Early 1900's. Mahogany veneer case. Ht. 15" W. 10½" . . $495.00

CANADA CLOCK CO. "Victoria" second style, no drawer. Hour and ½-hour strike, cupids & mirrors (Flying horse finials not original) Ht. 22½" $1850.00

RARE PARLOUR CLOCK. By George B Owen. 8-day with strike. Drawer in base for key. Ht. 22" $1400.00

ENGLISH TIMEPIECE. 8-day fusee pendulum movement, Ca. 1850. On dial John Bennett, Tunbridge Wells. Octagonal rosewood case with brass inlay. Diam. 16" $695.00

ANSONIA WALL CLOCK. Ca. 1885. 8-day, hour strike, 12" pendulum. Oak dial, 12" diam., applied brass numerals. $600.00

FRENCH FRAME CLOCK. Ca. 1850. 15-day, hour and ½-hour strike. Ebonized wood case with mother-of-pearl inlay and painted scene. 10" alabaster dail, porcelain numerals. Movement in wood box. Case, 15" square $695.00

OFFICE CLOCK. Seth Thomas 8-day, time only in oak case. Early 1900's. Ht. 23" $325.00

INGRAHAM. 8-day, hour strike, Ca. 1880. T.L. Coughlin, St. John, N.B. on label inside. Ht. 36" Width 15" $645.00

NO. 4 HANGING OFFICE REGULATOR Ithaca Calendar Clock by E.N. Welch, Ca. 1870. Nickel plate 31 day double mainspring movement. 12" time dial, 9" calendar dial. Ht. 29" All original. $2400.00

NOTE: Patented by H.B. Horton in 1866 who formed the Ithaca Clock Co. and sold calendar movements to various clock manufacturers.

SESSIONS WALL CLOCK. 8-day, hour and ½-hour strike, Ca. 1903. Oak case, copper fittings, glass with silver illustration. Ht. 23" W. 11" All original. $395.00

SESSIONS. Miniature 8-day school-room clock. Oak case, dial diam. 8" Early 1900's, all original. Ht. 19" $395.00

JEROME & CO. STEEPLE CLOCK.
Ca. 1890. 30-hour, hour strike.
Mahogany veneer case.
Ht. 15" W. 8½" $300.00

JEROME & CO. STEEPLE CLOCK.
Ca. 1865. 30-hour with alarm.
Mahogany veneer case with original
glass. Ht. 15" W. 8" $325.00

8-DAY STEEPLE CLOCK. Alarm
and strike on gong.
Ht. 20" $425.00

ANSONIA STEEPLE CLOCK. 8-
day, strike on gong.
Original glass. $425.00

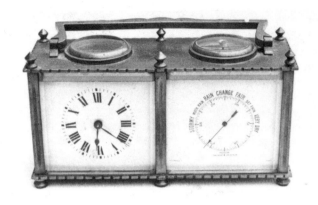

FRENCH ARMY OFFICER'S CLOCK. Carriage type clock and barometer with compass on top. Outer leather case missing.
Rare clock, Ca. 1912 . . . . $1250.00

FRENCH CARRIAGE CLOCK.
8-day with alarm, lever escapement.
Ht. 6" $950.00

FRENCH CARRIAGE CLOCK.
Cylinder movement in brass case with alarm. Ca. 1880 . . $600.00

WALTHAM. Size 10, 30-hour, key-wind movement, Ca. 1885.
With milk glass dial on marble base. Night clock fits on gas jet,
which, when lit, illuminates the dial so time can be seen.
Diam. of dial 4½" Base 6" x 5" Came in velvet case.
All original. $1200.00

WATERBURY. Ca. 1870. 8-day,
hour strike on bell. Wood and
bronze case with figures of
Esmeralda and her Goat.
Ht. 18" W. 15"
Mint $1500.00

POOLE ELECTRIC BATTERY
CLOCK. Early 1930's. The Poole
Mfg. Co. Inc., Ithaca, N.Y.
Mahogany veneer case, silver dial.
Ht. 10" W. 8"
All original $400.00

E.N. WELCH MFG. CO. 8-day, hour
strike. Ca. 1865. Iron case in the
oriental style decorated with mother-
of-pearl and nautical scene.
Ht. 18½" W. 12" $750.00

ANSONIA CLOCK, Ca. 1885.
8-day, hour and ½-hour strike.
In black cast iron case with
gilded ornamentation.
Ht. 10½" W. 9½" $375.00

WATERBURY. Ca. 1895. 8-day, time only. In copper plated
iron case by Jenning Bros., Bridgeport, Conn.
Ht. 8" L. 12" $500.00
NOTE: Jennings Bros. manufactured desk sets and mantel ornaments etc.

COTTAGE CLOCK. 30-hour timepiece. Maker unknown. Ca. 1870.
Ht. 11¾" $335.00

COTTAGE CLOCK. E. Ingraham
Co., 8-day, strike on gong. Original
tablet. Ca. 1895. - 1900. $535.00

COTTAGE CLOCK. Seth Thomas
8-day timepiece. Rosewood veneer
case. Ca. 1880. All original.
Ht. 9½" $300.00

COTTAGE CLOCK. Newhaven,
8-day with strike. Rosewood case,
original dial and tablet. Ca. 1880.
Ht. 15½" $750.00

KITCHEN CLOCK. E.N. Welch, 8-day, strike on gong with regulator pendulum. Original glass. Ca. 1875. Ht. 23" $425.00

CABINET CLOCK. Ansonia, Newark model. 8-day with strike. Ht. 18½" $650.00

KITCHEN CLOCK. E. Ingraham Minerva model. 8-day with strike and calendar. Original glass. Ht. 22" $400.00

HANGING KITCHEN CLOCK. Ansonia, 8-day with strike. Ht. 25" $495.00

Left —
SESSIONS. 8-day, strikes hour on gong, ½-hour on bell. Polished black wood case with brass fittings. Early 1900's.
Ht. 11" W. 15" $350.00

Right —
SESSIONS. "Wabash" 8-day, strikes hour on gong. Polished black wood case, marbelized mouldings and brass fittings.
Ca. 1915.
Ht. 11¾" W. 16" $400.00

Left —
ANSONIA. 8-day, hour and ½-hour strike on gong. In cast iron case with brass fittings. Ca. 1885.
Ht. 11" W. 16" $450.00

Left —
SESSIONS "DAWSON"
Ca. 1913. 8-day, hour
and ½-hour strike. Case
stained mahogany with
brass fittings.
Ht. 10½"
W. 17½"   . . $300.00

Right —
NEWHAVEN "AUTHOR"
Ca. 1917, 8-day, hour and
½-hour strike. Mahogany
case, paper dial. Ht. 9½"
L. 15" $300.00

Left —
SETH THOMAS. Ca. 1910.
8-day, strike on gong, dial
regulation. Mahogany veneer
case, floral marquetry decoration and brass bun feet.
Ht. 13" W. 9" $300.00

DINING SET. Walnut, by North American Furniture Co., Owen Sound, Ont. Late 1920's, early 1930's. Table with two drop-in leaves, five side chairs, one arm chair. Table dimension without leaves 52" x 42" Refinished.   Set $1195.00

FURNITURE

HARVEST TABLE. Pine, two drawers have been replaced. Ca. 1890. Length 8 ft. x 34" wide. $850.00
MATCHING PRESSED BACK CHAIRS. Ca. 1910.
Set of six. Each 145.00

Left —
CARD TABLE. Mahogany, swivel top with green baize surface. Inlaid with ebony, carved acanthus leaf pedestal and legs on brass casters. American Regency period, Ca. 1800. Ht. 29"
Table open 36" x 36" . . $3650.00

Right —
GAMES TABLE, tilt top. Walnut inlaid with mixed woods, chess board and geometric pattern. Carved pedestal on tripod base. Ht. 24" Diam. 27"
1920's. $1000.00

Not Shown —
CANDLE/LAMP TABLE. Round tilt-top with checker board painted on surface. Turned pedestal, quad spider leg base. $595.00
CANDLE/LAMP TABLE. With small drawer. Turned column on tripod base. Ca. 1860. . . . . . . 675.00

Not Shown —
KITCHEN TABLE. Tiger maple, three plank top, one drawer, tapered legs, H-stretcher. Ca. 1840's. 50" x 37"
As found. $1750.00
WORK TABLE. Butternut and birdseye maple. Sheraton style, two drawers. Ca. 1840. . . . . . 775.00

Left —
WALNUT TABLE. Canted corners, carved and turned columns and legs, inverted vase finial. Ca. 1910. 31" x 29" x 22" $1100.00

WORK/CANDLE TABLE. Decorated with marquetry and inlaid mother-of-pearl surrounding key hole. Turned column on tripod base. Ht. 30" Top 17" x 15½" $650.00

TILT-TOP TABLE. Black papier-mache top, diam. 19" inlaid with mother-of-pearl and painted floral decoration. Base also with mother-of-pearl inlay. Ca. 1860. Ht. 26" $850.00

DUMB WAITER. Hepplewhite, Ca. 1780. Mahogany, two tier, lion paw feet on casters. Ht. 39" Lower table, diam. 26" Upper table, diam. 20" $2375.00

WALNUT TABLE. Turned pedestal on platform base. Ca. 1880. Ht. 30." Diam. 24" $550.00

KITCHEN CUPBOARD. Decorated central cupboard door. All original. 88" x 52" x 24" $1200.00

MOTHERS HELPER. Oak by Chatham Furniture Co., Ca. 1904. Upper cupboard doors with pebbled glass, mirror in central door. Originally had extension leaves at each side. 64" x 44" x 26" $1295.00

FLAT-TO-THE-WALL. Pine, from Quebec, original blue paint. 82" x 52" x 26" $1200.00

PRESERVE CUPBOARD. Pine, from Quebec, Ca. 1840. Original square nails. 70" x 36" x 14" $750.00

WELSH DRESSER. Oak, made in Britain, 1930's.
70" x 43" x 16" $1150.00

COURT CUPBOARD. Oak, deco style. Late 1920's, early 1930's.
56" x 42" x 19" $995.00

OAK BUFFET. Upper cupboard with coloured leaded glass door. Bevelled mirror.
78" x 54" x 19" $995.00

SIDEBOARD. Pine, from Quebec.
65" x 52" x 19" $775.00

ICE BOX. Oak, Frigidaire, Ca. 1910.
Brass hardware, two door handles
missing.
43" x 26" x 24" $535.00

ICE BOX. Oak. Lift top over ice
compartment, original hardware.
Small repair to base, refinished.
45" x 30" x 20" $675.00

Left —
BUCKET BENCH.
From western Ontario, Ca. 1860.
All original, including green paint.
Ht. 40" w. 38" $695.00

STONEWARE —
Top — Left — Jug, "H. Black,
Stirling, Ont." $120.00
Top — Right — Jug,
"Markdale" 175.00
Middle — Left — 6 gallon
crock 485.00
Middle — Right — 2 gallon
jug. 395.00
Bottom — Left — 2 gallon
crock. (chipped) 275.00
Bottom — Right — 1 gallon
jug, Brantford. 185.00

WALNUT PLANT STAND.
Turned pedestal. Ca. 1880.
41" high $135.00

WALNUT PLANT STAND.
Ca. 1870.
43" high. $115.00

PLANT STAND. Inlay
decoration.
36" high. $125.00

OAK PLANT STAND.
Ca. 1900.
42" high. $100.00

PIANO STOOL. Turned legs and
stretchers, dolphin feet. $235.00

PIANO STOOL. Carved tripod
base. $185.00

DRESSING TABLE STOOL.
Cane seat. $95.00

JOINT STOOL. Oak, Ca. 1850.
Pegged construction. $260.00

HALL STAND. Eastlake style.
Walnut, turn of the century.
Ht. 78" $650.00

DISPLAY CABINET. Ca. 1910.
New brass pulls.
40" x 21" x 10" $615.00

SWING DRESSING MIRROR.
Walnut frame and stand, fitted
with good quality mirror,
panelled back.
Ht. 18" $135.00

HALL STAND. Oak, box seat
with hinged lid. Full size mirror
replaced with small square.
71" x 26" x 13½" . . $160.00

HIGH CHAIR. Made from a stool. Low back Windsor style with comb. Ca. 1860. Ht. 33" $195.00

HIGH CHAIR. Pine. $100.00

ROCKING CHAIR. Wood and wicker. Ca. 1900. Ht. 35" $225.00

HIGH CHAIR. Wood and wicker with rush seat, dark stained. Ca. 1900. Ht. 28" $250.00

PLANTATION CHAIRS. Thought to have been made by slaves. Mahogany with upholstered seats and arm rests. Backs are hand carved from a single piece of wood. Ca. 1840. Pair $895.00

Not Shown —
CHAIR. Windsor with bamboo turned legs and spindles, shaped crest rail, H-stretcher. Marked on bottom of seat "J. Humeston, Halifax, Warranted" . . . . $ 875.00
CHAIRS. Windsor, arrowback. Refinished. Set of 5 . . . . . .   950.00
COUCH. Wood with cushion seat. Spool turned arms and spindles, solid back, turned legs. 1500.00

LOVE SEAT. Victoria, Eastlake style. Elm frame, gold velvet upholstery. $245.00

MORRIS CHAIR. Oak frame, velvet cushion.
Ht. 43" $350.00

SECRETARY/BOOKCASE. Butternut. Fitted interior includes two lamp supports and secret drawer. Drawers and cupboards below writing surface, upper doors with original glass.
88" x 54" x 21" $2500.00

SECRETARY/BOOKCASE. Quarter cut oak. Made by Macey, Hamilton, Ont., 1915 - 20. Drop front desk with fitted interior with drawer and cupboard below. Upper section, three stacking book cases with leaded glass doors.
82" x 34" x 17" $3295.00

Not Shown —
WALL SHELF. Original alligatored red paint, three drawers. From Niagara Peninsula.
Ca. 1880.   . . . . $435.00
UMBRELLA/CANE STAND.
European, Ca. 1850.   . . . . 750.00

Left —
SECRETARY/BOOKCASE. Ontario Ca. 1860. Basswood and mahogany. Glazed bookcase doors, fitted interior over writing surface.
85" x 39" x 20" $1995.00

SLANT FRONT DESK. Oak, deco style with original fitted leather writing surface. $800.00

OAK DESK. English, Ca. 1900. Drop front desk with fitted interior, leather writing surface. All original. 54" x 49" x 16" $950.00

OAK WRITING BOX. Fitted interior with compartments for pens, pencils, ink and stationery etc. Ht. 10" $110.00

STACKING BOOKCASE. Four section. Oak, glazed doors, one compartment with drawer. English. 60" x 34" x 11" $1150.00

CORNER WASHSTAND. English, Ca. 1860. Mahogany with marble top. Ht. 28" $350.00

WASHSTAND. Basswood and pine. Ca. 1880. 35" x 30" x 17" $275.00

WASHSTAND. Maple, Ca. 1920. 48" x 29" x 17" $175.00

WASHSTAND Oak, new drawer pulls. 36" x 28" x 16" $265.00

WASHSTAND. Ash, late 1800's. With candle/lamp shelves, original teardrop drawer pulls. Refinished.
36" x 29" x 15" $295.00

CHEST-OF-DRAWERS. Ash, Empire style, from Brant County, Ontario. All original, excellent condition.
48" x 44" x 20" $695.00

GENTLEMAN'S WARDROBE. Oak with four corner shelves, acorn handles. 1930's.
52" x 33" x 18" $695.00

CHEST-OF-DRAWERS/COMMODE. Probably French, Ca. 1880. Bombe shape, decorated with marquetry. All original, with marble top.
39" x 17" x 13" $2800.00

Left —
STORAGE CHEST. Pine,
refinished, lift-top, bracket
base. Ca. 1870.
42" x 25½" x 22" $245.00

Right —
STORAGE CHEST.
Pine, refinished,
lift-top, moulded
base. Ca. 1880
38" x 18"
x 15½" $275.00

Left —
STORAGE CHEST. Pine,
lift-top, brass fittings.
36" x 17" x 17" $195.00

Right —
TRUNK/STORAGE CHEST.
Pine and oak, metal strapping
and fittings, leather handles.
36" x 20½" x 23" $250.00

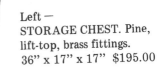

CANDLE HOLDERS. Wood, hand made. Break-down and fit into bases which form a box when put together. Ht. 2¼" Diam. 4½" Pair . . $45.00

Not Shown —
JEWEL BOX.
Basswood inlaid with mother-of-pearl. Ca. 1840. $395.00

KNIFE BOX/CASE. Sheraton style, serpentine front, bracket feet, decorated with silver inlay. Late 1700's - early 1800's. Interior converted and fitted to store stationery. $1450.00

SPINNING WHEEL. British, early 1800's. Unusual design. Ht. with distaff 45" $325.00

Left —
TIN BATH. Rolled edges.
Width 31" $145.00

Right —
TIN BATH. Green with
gold stripe, cream
interior. Ca. 1870.
L. 29" $95.00

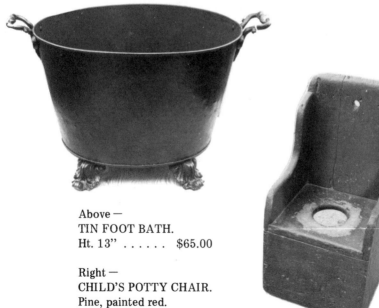

Above —
TIN FOOT BATH.
Ht. 13" $65.00

Right —
CHILD'S POTTY CHAIR.
Pine, painted red.
Ht. 23" 185.00

FURNITURE – Not Shown –

BED. Four poster. Tiger maple, Ca. 1850. Width 54" $3350.00

BLANKET BOX/CHEST. Transitional. Painted pine, one drawer, wood pulls, lift top to upper storage section, shaped base, some restoration. 475.00

BLANKET BOX/ STORAGE CHEST. Painted blue, moulded base. 275.00

BUFFET. Pine, five graduated drawers each side of central cupboard doors, wood pulls, bracket base. Ca. 1850. L. 62" 1475.00

CHAIR. Windsor with writing arm with small drawer. American, Ca. 1830. . . . . 1450.00

CHEST/BONNET. From Quebec, two glove drawers flanked with bonnet drawers, three full length drawers below. Wood pulls, cock beading on drawers. 1495.00

CHEST OF DRAWERS. Cherry, from Ontario, Ca. 1870. Bracket base, five drawers. 625.00

CHEST OF DRAWERS. Cherry, from Ontario, Ca. 1870. Two small upper drawers with three full length drawers below, wood pulls. . . 875.00

CHILD'S CHAIR. Stick chair with solid pine seat. Ca. 1900 . . . . 95.00

CHILD'S FLAT-TO-THE-WALL. Painted pine. Broken arch pediment, with finials. Ca. 1900. Ht. 36" 325.00

CHILD'S FLAT-TO-THE-WALL. Step-back with two cupboard doors in upper section, two drawers with cupboard in lower storage section. Ca. 1900. . . . . 675.00

COBBLER'S BENCH. 275.00

CRADLE. Solid shaped board sides, no hood, painted red. 350.00

CRADLE. Solid sides with hood, rocker. 495.00

CUPBOARD. Armoire, panelled doors. 6500.00

CUPBOARD. Corner, brown finish, blind doors, two up, two down. 2300.00

CUPBOARD. Corner, painted pine, two glazed upper doors, two drawers and cupboard in lower storage section. 3600.00

CUPBOARD. Corner, pine from Quebec, Ca. 1830. One door in upper section with nine panes of glass, two cupboard doors in lower storage section. Some restoration. 8500.00

CUPBOARD. Flat-to-the-wall. Glazed gothic arched upper doors, lower doors and side panels decorated with gothic panels. Ca. 1850. 2350.00

CUPBOARD. Flat-to-the-wall. Two glazed upper doors, two drawers with two cupboards in lower section, original paint. Ca. 1920. . . . . 2350.00

CUPBOARD. Flat-to-the-wall. Ukranian from Manitoba, original finish. Two glazed upper doors, flatware drawer and two cupboard doors in lower storage section. Ca. 1900. . . . . 1650.00

CUPBOARD. Linen from Quebec. Refinished pine, shaped skirt, panelled doors, Ca. 1830. . . . . 3500.00

FURNITURE — Not Shown —

DESK. Butler's. Figured maple veneer, drop front, fitted interior,
three full length drawers below writing surface. $2850.00

DESK. Davenport. Rosewood, with Queen Anne legs on casters,
three side drawers, brass pulls. 2200.00

DESK. Davenport. Walnut with inlay, four drawers, lift top.
English, Ca. 1830. Excellent condition. 4250.00

DESK. Slant front. Flamed mahogany from New Brunswick, Ca. 1880.
Fitted interior, four drawers below writing surface, glass pulls,
ornately turned legs. 975.00

DESK. Slant front. Small, pine, American. One single drawer below
writing surface, interior fitted with drawers and compartments,
tapered legs. Ca. 1900. . . . . 985.00

DESK. Standing. Butternut and birch, lift top, one drawer, turned legs
and stretchers, shaped gallery board, wood pulls. Ca. 1840. . . . . 2500.00

DRY SINK. With two cupboard doors below, shelf above with three
drawers. 1850.00

HALL STAND/SEAT. Oak, lift up seat over storage area, ornate
applied carving. 2195.00

HALL STAND/SEAT. Oak, lift up seat over storage area, decorated
with applied carving and cut outs. Ca. 1890. . . . . 1595.00

SETTEE. Pine and maple, Ca. 1850. Shaped crest rail, spool turned
spindles and legs. 1175.00

SIDEBOARD. Welsh, mahogany. Five deep square drawers, one
cupboard door, brass pulls, bun feet. 1300.00

SOFA. Mahogany frame. Upholstered in rose velvet with central
diamond tufted medallion. English, Ca. 1840. . . . . 3500.00

STORAGE BENCH. Shaped back, turned arm rest, painted yellow
with black lift-up seat over storage section. Mennonite from western
Canada. 1350.00

TABLE. Kitchen, pegged top, turned legs, three drawers with wood
pulls. From Waterloo County. Ca. 1860. . . . . 1600.00

TABLE. Kitchen, walnut pegged top, turned legs, two drawers with
wood pulls. Cal 1840. . . . . 3750.00

TABLE. Sawbuck. Length 48" 750.00

TABLE. Tea/Card. Mahogany, from Maritimes, Ca. 1830. Fold-over
top, turned legs. 1345.00

TABLE. Work/Candle. Walnut, from Waterloo County, Ca. 1840.
Two drawers, drop leaf, brass pulls and casters. 875.00

UMBRELLA STAND. Oak, footed. 85.00

GLASS

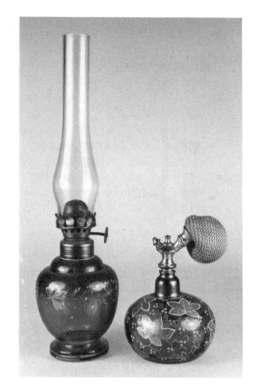

CRANBERRY: A lovely wine-red glass used alone or with glass of another colour for tableware, lamps and a wide variety of decorative pieces.

Left — LAMP. Cranberry glass, decorated with gold. Ht. 9½"   . . $350.00
Right — PERFUME BOTTLE. Cranberry decorated with enamel and gold. Ht. 4½" 285.00

PICKLE CASTER. Cranberry insert. Silver plate frame made in Canada by Wm. Rogers. Ht. 10½" $365.00

SALT & PEPPER. Cranberry glass decorated with enamel and gold, silver plate tops. Ht. 3½"
Pair $190.00

OPEN SALTS.
Left — Cranberry with clear fan feet and handle. Ht. 2" . . $150.00
Right — Cranberry, cut to clear, rayed base. Ht. 3" 150.00

COVERED CANDY DISHES. Cranberry with clear finials and rigaree.
Left — Ht. 4½" . . . . $325.00   Right — Ht. 5½" $450.00

RIGAREE: Applied ruffles of glass in the same colour as the body or in a contrasting shade.

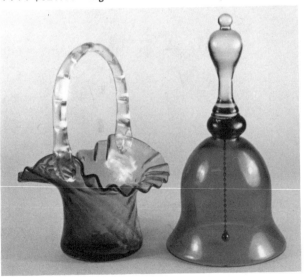

Left —
CRANBERRY
BASKET.
Clear handle.
Ht. 6" $100.00

Right —
CRANBERRY
BELL.
Clear handle.
Ht. 7½" $200.00

CRANBERRY GLASS PITCHERS — Left to Right —
Clear handle and feet. Ht. 3½" $120.00
Clear handle. Ht. 3¾" 150.00
Clear handle. Ht. 5" 165.00

CRANBERRY GLASS VASES.
Left & Right — Enamel decoration, ribbon edge, silver plate
bases. Ht. 4" .... Pair .. $450.00
Centre — Enamel decoration, gold trim, Sheffield plate base.
Ht. 7" 275.00

CRANBERRY GLASS VASES. Decorated with gold and flowers.
Left — Ht. 3" . . . . . . $250.00   Right — Ht. 5" $275.00

Left — CRANBERRY GLASS CORDIALS. Enamel and gold decoration,
clear handles. Ht. 1¾" . . . .   Pair . . $225.00
Right — CRANBERRY GLASS CORDIALS. Enamel and gold decoration.
Ht. 2¾" . . . .   Pair . . 225.00

CRANBERRY
GLASS —
Left to Right —
Cup.
Ht. 2" $ 95.00
Mug.
Ht. 2¼"   120.00
Mug, decorated
with gold and
enamel.
Ht. 3½"   200.00

WATER PITCHER. Cranberry/
opalescent. Clear celery handle.
Ht. 9" $495.00

SYRUP JUG. Cranberry/opal-
escent, clear celery handle.
Silver plated mount and
lid. $365.00

ICE BUCKET. Cranberry/
opalescent. Mount and handle
requires replating. $250.00

CREAMER. Cranberry/opal-
escent. Ht. 4" $175.00

LEMONADE SET. Cranberry glass decorated with white, pink and turquoise flowers. Late 1800's.
Pitcher 9½" high.
Set $950.00

PICKLE CASTOR. Cranberry thumbprint insert, enamel flowers. Toronto Silver Plate frame with fork.
Late 1800's. $475.00

VICTORIAN CANDY/SAUCE DISH. Vaseline blown glass bowl in gilded brass stand with cupids.
Length 8" $265.00

123

EPERGNE. Cranberry glass with applied clear glass frills. Large centre vase with three small vases. Ht. 21" $650.00

EPERGNE. Clear, opalescent and cranberry glass. Large centre vase with three baskets hanging from twisted glass arms.
Ht. 23" $1250.00

EPERGNE: Centrepiece, used as a table ornament to hold flowers or fruit.

Not Shown —
EPERGNE. Ca. 1890. Vaseline and white opalescent glass with four trumpet shaped vases, one large, three small. $595.00
JACK-IN-THE-PULPIT VASE. Vaseline, opalescent and blue glass. 245.00

Left —
EPERGNE. Silver plate figural stand. Quilted glass dishes, clear to flame. Late 1800's. Ht. 16" $750.00

Mary Gregory Glass

The young lady who was believed to have originated the paintings of children on this attractive glassware was a decorator in the lamp department of the Boston & Sandwich Glass Company from 1880 - 1884. Rural scenes, rather than children, were most often used as decoration. No one would be more surprised than Miss Gregory herself to find that her name had been associated with this European glassware. Probably nobody will ever know for sure how the myth started, but a change of name seems unlikely.

The earlier pieces, which date from about 1895 to the early 1900's, are superior in quality and detail of decoration to later mass produced copies. The examples illustrated here are all from the earlier period.

PITCHER. Green with clear celery handle. Ht. 7½" $450.00

LEMONADE GLASS. Iridized pale amber, inverted thumbprint pattern.
Ht. 5" $200.00
PITCHER. Iridized pale amber.
Ht. 9¾" 575.00

LEMONADE PITCHER.
Emerald green.
Ht. 13" $675.00

DECANTER. Royal blue, clear applied handle, cut glass stopper not original. "Liqueur Surfine, P. Bardinet, Limoges." Ht. 8½" $275.00

DECANTER. Emerald green, clear blown stopper, applied handle. Small chip at spout. Ht. 12" $50.00

DECANTER. Vaseline with clear applied handle and cut glass stopper. Ht. 9½" $650.00

JUICE TUMBLER. Smokey amber. Ht. 4¼" $175.00
JUICE TUMBLER. Amethyst 175.00
JUICE TUMBLER. Cranberry. 250.00

Left to Right —
CORDIAL,
amber.
Ht. 3" $145.00
SHOT GLASS,
green. 125.00
SHOT GLASS,
amber. 135.00

FOOTED TUMBLERS —
Left to Right —
Apple green, gold trim,
clear foot and stem.
Ht. 5½" $150.00
Sapphire, gold trim.
Ht. 6½" 175.00
Cranberry.
Ht. 5¾" 225.00

Left — VASE. Green, gold trim.
Ht. 12½" $400.00
Right — VASE. Cobalt, boy's
cheeks and hands are coloured
pink. Ht. 10" 400.00

VASES. Frosted apple green.
Ht. 9" . . . . Pair $625.00

BUD VASES — Left to Right —
Cranberry. Ht. 5¾" $425.00
Green with clear rigaree. Ht. 6¾" 375.00
Cobalt. Ht. 4" 325.00

PITCHERS — GIRL & BOY. Frosted green shading to clear. Clear applied handles, gold trim. Children's cheeks, hands and arms are coloured pink. Ht. 11" . . . . Each . . $400.00

BLOWN LAMP. Green.
Ht. 10" $675.00

CHEESE BELL. Clear with boy on one side, girl on the other. Pink coloured hands and faces. Base not original.
Diam. 7" Ht. 7½" $450.00

PERFUME BOTTLES — Left to Right —
Blue shading to clear. Baby Thumbprint pattern. Ht. 5" . . $275.00
Clear bottle, blue trim on dress. Ht. 7¼" 165.00
Diamond shaped bottle, cut glass stopper. Some blue and
green colouring in decoration. 350.00
Octagonal bottle. Clear. Ht. 5" 150.00

Left — BOTTLE. Emerald green, decorated with white and gold. Blown
stopper. Ht. 9½" $300.00
Right — BOTTLE. Baby blue, gold
trim, tulip stopper. Ht. 11"   425.00

Left — BARBER BOTTLE. Amber
with matching blown stopper.
Ht. 8" $475.00
Right — BARBER BOTTLE. Deep
green, clear stopper not original.
Ht. 7½" 325.00

Left — SPILL HOLDER. French opaline and blue with metal
base. Ht. 4" $225.00
Right — JELLY/JAM JAR. Cased blue. Ht. 5" 325.00

Not Shown — Glass with Mary Gregory type decoration.
PITCHER. Clear, ruffled top, applied celery handle. Ht. 8¾" $450.00
PITCHER. Emerald green, ruffled top, applied handle. Ht. 7½" .. 435.00
POWDER BOX. Electric blue, brass fittings, signed A.H. Ht. 8" .. 975.00
STEMWARE. Cordial, clear with knob stem. Ht. 3¾" 135.00
STEMWARE. Wine, blue with gold trim. Ht. 5½" 195.00
TUMBLER. Green. Ht. 4¼" 165.00

PATCH BOXES — Both trimmed with gold.
Left — Cranberry. Diam. 2½" Ht. 2" $400.00
Right — Pale green. Diam. 2" Ht. 1½" 300.00

In the early 1960's the decanter of Remy Martin Cognac was sold packed in a wicker carrying case.

Height including stopper 11"

DECANTER. On base —
"E. Remy Martin & Cie, Cognac, France. "
"Made in France by Baccarat"
An exact replica of a flask discovered on the site of a battle fought at Jarnac in 1569. Remy Martin acquired the flask and had it copied as a container for his rare Cognacs. The original flask was given to a Paris museum. The Cristallierie de Baccarat has been making these decanters since 1920. Remy Martin Louis XIII Grande Champagne Cognac is still sold in this type of decanter.
Value of decanter $400.00
A decanter containing this fine Cognac would cost about $1350.00 today.

Left —
SAMOVAR.
Cambridge Glass "Molly" pattern. Azure blue, machine etched grape and vine. Nickel plated fittings. Early 1930's. Ht. 15"
Mint. $350.00

Cigarette Holders

CIGARETTE HOLDERS — Ca. 1930.
Left — Bohemian glass, flashed ruby, etched and cut to clear. Ht. 3½" $55.00
Right — Black amethyst glass with silver overlay. Ht. 2¾" 35.00

CIGARETTE HOLDERS — 1920's. - 30's.
Left — Apple green glass, silverplate cage with match strike. Ht. 4"   . . $55.00
Right — Dark amber with silverplate cage and match strike. Ht. 2½" . .   45.00

CIGARETTE HOLDERS —
Left — Porcelain studio piece, signed "E. David." American Ca. 1910. Knave of spades, black interior and base. Ht. 4" $45.00
Right — Ceramic cigarette holder/ash tray. Blue, yellow and orange. Japanese. Ht. 4" 30.00

CIGARETTE HOLDERS — Left to Right —
Clear, silver and white trim. Ht. 3¼" $30.00
Clear. Ht. 4" 22.00
Clear, Duncan & Miller's Spiral Flutes pattern with cameo and flower basket
silver overlay. Ht. 4¼" 30.00

CIGARETTE HOLDERS.
Duncan & Miller's Spiral
Flutes pattern.
Left — Amber, decorated
with etched lines. $35.00
Right — Amber, trimmed
with silver and decorated
with silver deposit sailing
ship. 30.00

CIGARETTE HOLDERS. Left to Right —
Amber, "Internal Ridge" Ht. 4¼" $35.00
Pink with remnants of hand painted decoration. Ht. 3¾" 35.00
Apple green, "External Ridge" Remnants of hand painted decoration. 30.00

CIGARETTE HOLDERS. Fostoria Glass Co., late 1920's. Bases are for used matches. Ht. 4" — Left to Right —

Forest green and clear. $55.00
Light amber and clear. 50.00
Cobalt blue and clear. 60.00

CIGARETTE HOLDERS. With ashtray base.
Left — Apple green. Diam. of base 6" ht. 4" $55.00
Right — Amber. Diam. of base 6" ht. 4" 55.00

CIGARETTE HOLDERS.
Left — Amethyst, clear base and stem. By Cambridge Glass Co.,
Ca. 1920. Ht. 4" . . . . $ 45.00
Right — Sapphire blue. Marked "Steuben Glass Shape 6264"
Ca. 1924. Ht. 5¼" 100.00

CIGARETTE HOLDERS. Ca. 1925.
Left — Pale amber, bulldog etched on both sides. Ht. 3½" $75.00
Right — Apple green, horse's head etched on both sides. Ht. 3½" . . 75.00

CIGARETTE HOLDER. Pink
glass with match box holder.
Patent date Nov. 16, 1926.
L. 4¼" Ht. 3" $50.00

CIGARETTE HOLDER. Pink
pressed glass. Indiana Glass Co.
Frosted Rose pattern. Ca. 1925.
Ht. 3¼" $25.00
In clear 20.00

PIPE ASH TRAY. Amber glass.
Patent date June 12, 1923.
American, maker unknown.
L. 6½" $30.00

Left to Right —
MATCH HOLDER/STRIKER. White pottery, glazed pink lustre base.
Ht. 3" $25.00
MATCH HOLDER/STRIKER. Pottery with blue and cream
glaze. 20.00
MATCH HOLDER/STRIKER. Cream with coat-of-arms decor-
ation. By Carlton Ware, Stoke-on-Trent, England. 40.00

Left —
VASELINE GLASS
TOOTHPICK OR
MATCH HOLDER.
Ca. 1900.
Ht. 2½" . . $30.00
Right —
NORITAKE MATCH
HOLDER. Decorated
with cigar and matches
on pale caramel ground.
Ht. 2" . . 42.00

MATCH HOLDER. Milk glass.
Ca. 1900. Ht. 2¾" . . $35.00

MATCH HOLDER/STRIKER.
Ribbed forest green glass.
Ca. 1910. Ht. 2¾" . . $25.00

Opalescent Glass

OPALESCENT GLASS: Translucent, iridescent, refracts light and reflects it in a play of colours. Blown and pressed glass, made by many glass houses in North America and Europe. Made in many forms such as, tableware, novelties, lamps and decorative pieces and found in a large range of colours, often with added hand painted decoration.

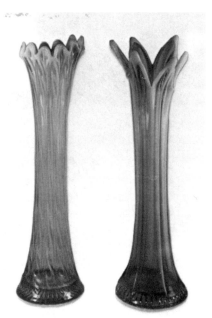

OPALESCENT GREEN VASES.
Left — Boggy Bayou pattern.
Ht. 12½" $70.00
Right — Ribbed pattern.
Ht. 13" 65.00

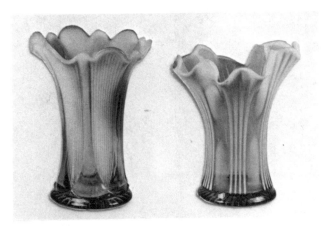

OPALESCENT BLUE SWEET PEA VASES.
Left — Lined Heart pattern. Ht. 7½" $65.00
Right — Long Thumbprint pattern. Ht. 6½" 75.00

Left — OPALESCENT GREEN CANDY DISH.
Maple Leaf Chalice pattern. Ht. 6¼" $150.00
Right — OPALESCENT GREEN VASE. With three handles.
Aurora Borealis pattern. Ht. 6" 65.00

OPALESCENT
GREEN FOOTED
CANDY BOWLS.
Left —
Spool pattern.
Ht. 4¾" . . $35.00
Right —
Hilltop Vines
pattern.
Ht. 4¾" . . 65.00

Left —
OPALESCENT
GREEN FOOTED
VASE.
Cabbage Leaf
pattern.
Ht. 6" . . $100.00
Right —
OPALESCENT
BLUE FOOTED
ROSE BOWL.
Opal Open
pattern.
Ht. 5" . . 90.00

Top — OPALESCENT BLUE ROSE BOWLS — Left to Right —
Daisy & Fan pattern. $150.00
Owl & Turkey Foot pattern. Ht. 4½" 100.00
Seaweed pattern. 150.00
Bottom — OPALESCENT BLUE FOOTED BOWLS.
Argonaut pattern. Left 3½" high. .... Each 110.00

Top — Left — OPALESCENT VASELINE FOOTED BOWL.
Fluted Scrolls pattern. Ht. 2" $60.00
Top — Right — OPALESCENT BLUE FOOTED BOWL.
Beaded Cable pattern. Ht. 2½" 65.00
Bottom — Left — OPALESCENT BLUE FOOTED BOWL.
Rings & Ruffles pattern. Ht. 3" 70.00
Bottom — Right — OPALESCENT GREEN FOOTED BOWL.
Iris with Meander pattern. Ht. 3½" 70.00

Top — OPALESCENT VASELINE BOWL.
Spear & Fan pattern. 8" x 2" $80.00
Bottom — Left — OPALESCENT BLUE BOWL.
Northwood Drapery pattern. Diam. 8" 75.00
Bottom — Right — OPALESCENT GREEN FOOTED BOWL.
Coral pattern. 65.00

Top — OPALESCENT BLUE FOOTED BOWLS.
Left — Vintage pattern. Ht. 3½" $70.00
Right — Button Panels pattern. Ht. 3" 75.00
Bottom — Left — OPALESCENT VASELINE FOOTED BOWL.
With cranberry chips. 95.00
Bottom — Right — OPALESCENT GREEN FOOTED BOWL.
Beaded Fleur-de-lis pattern. Ht. 4½" 75.00

141

CHILDRENS' MUGS.

Top — Left
Waterfowl pattern. Ca. 1890. $45.00

Centre — Left —
Beaded Circle pattern.
Ht. 3¼" $45.00

Bottom — Left —
Ball & Swirl pattern. $45.00

Top — Right —
Diamond Band pattern.   . . $60.00

Centre — Right —
Log & Star pattern
Ht. 2½" $40.00

Bottom — Right —
New York Pattern.
McKee Glass. $50.00

Wavecrest

The C.F. Monroe Co., Meriden Conn. used three trade names on their products — WAVECREST, KELVA and NAKARA. All three of these wares were made in rich extravagant styles with fine enamel decoration applied to the creamy opal glass. The line included items such as, dressing table sets, humidors, jardinieres and cookie jars etc.

WAVECREST.
Left — Bud Vase. Blue with floral decoration and ormolu foot and rim.
Ht. 5" $275.00
Right — Covered Box. White decorated with a rural scene on lid. Ca. 1910.
Ht. 3" Diam. 3¼"   345.00

Right — JEWEL BOX.
Marked Kelva. Marbelized, mat finish, floral decoration.
Ht. 2¾" Diam. 5" $500.00

TRINKET BOXES. Ca. 1900.
Left — Marked Nakara. Ht. 2" Diam. 4" $275.00
Right — Marked Wavecrest. Shell pattern. Ht. 3" Diam. 4¼" . . 400.00

WAVECREST TRINKET BOXES. Ca. 1900.
Left — Swirl pattern, floral decoration. Ht. 2¾" Diam. 4" $375.00
Right — Swirl pattern, floral decoration. Ht. 3" Diam. 4½" 250.00

WAVECREST HANDLED OPEN TRAYS.
Left — Rococo pattern, floral decoration. Ht. 1¾" Diam. 3½" .. $135.00
Right — Egg crate pattern, floral decoration. Ht. 2¼" 225.00

WAVECREST.
Left — Hair Tidy, rococo pattern, floral decoration. Ht. 2½" .. $325.00
Right — Trinket Tray, painted cats. Ht. 1½" Diam. 3" Ca. 1910   145.00

WAVECREST TRINKET TRAYS.
Left — Seashell pattern, floral decoration. Ht. 1½" Diam. 3" .. $195.00
Right — Swirl pattern, floral decoration. Ht. 1¾" Diam. 4½" .. 145.00

Left —
WAVECREST. Letter or photograph container. Pale blue egg crate pattern with floral decoration and ormolu mount.
6" x 4½" x 3" $525.00

Right —
WAVECREST. Ferner.
Rare hexagon shape,
decorated with flowers.
Gilded brass liner.
Ht. 4" Diam. 8" $650.00

Left —
WAVECREST. Ferner.
Pale blue, rococo pattern
with floral decoration.
Diam. 7" $400.00

CRUETS and SHAKERS

TWO BOTTLE CRUET SET. Bullseye pattern, opaque white, hand painted decoration. Ht. 4½" $150.00

THREE BOTTLE CRUET SET. Hand painted floral decoration on milk glass, fan base. Ca. 1885 - 90. Ht. 7" $120.00

THREE BOTTLE CRUET SET. Bulging Petal pattern, powder blue cased glass. Ca. 1880's. Ht. 8" $225.00

MILK GLASS SHAKER. Barrel shape. $20.00
MILK GLASS SHAKER. Floral decoration. Ht. 3¼" 20.00
MILK GLASS SHAKER. Floral decoration. 20.00

MILK GLASS SHAKER. Cosmos Scroll (Petite Fleur) $20.00
MILK GLASS SHAKER. Fatima Scroll. Ht. 2¾" 20.00
MILK GLASS SHAKER. Pansy, hand painted. 45.00

Left — SALT & PEPPER SHAKERS. Opal glass with hand painted decoration. By Mount Washington Glass Co. Pair . . . . $ 95.00
Right — SHAKERS. Not a pair — Crown Milano pattern by Mount Washington Glass Co. Each 150.00

MILK GLASS SHAKER. Thistle & Fern $30.00
MILK GLASS SHAKER. Wavecrest, rare, Ca. 1910. Ht. 3" 85.00
MILK GLASS SHAKER. Fan 22.00

MILK GLASS SHAKER. Pattern not known. $20.00
MILK GLASS SHAKER. Wild Iris. Ht. 3½" 30.00
MILK GLASS SHAKER. Beaded Panel. 25.00

MILK GLASS SHAKER. Corn. $45.00
MILK GLASS SHAKER. Grape & Leaf. Ht. 3¾" 25.00
MILK GLASS SHAKER. Rope. 20.00

SHAKER. Block & Sunburst. Opaque blue. $45.00
SHAKER. Alternating Rib. Cased pink. Ht. 3½" 45.00
SHAKER. Creased Bale. Opaque blue. 40.00

SHAKER. Coralene on opal Bristol glass. $45.00
SHAKER. Floral pattern, opaque green. 45.00
SHAKER. Beaded Dahlia, opaque green. 65.00

SHAKER. Leaf Overlapping. Cased pink. $53.00
SHAKER. Bulging Petal. Cased blue. Ht. 2¼" 40.00
SHAKER. Cord & Tassel. Opaque green. 55.00

Numbered Shakers

Salts and peppers in opaque white and blue are listed by numbers only, one two twelve, in the 1902 catalogue of the Diamond Glass Co., Limited, Montreal, Quebec. Shards in white and blue of numbered shakers were found at the Burlington Glass Works site, Hamilton, Ontario.

The numbers are embossed on the base, but shakers are also found without numbers. Salts and peppers in these designs were often decorated with hand painting and are now and then seen with remnants of this decoration.

Left to Right —
Oak Leaf & Inverted Fleur-de-lis. (No. 2) Ht. 2½" . . . . $30 - $40
Canadian Moon & Star. (No.3) Ht. 2½" . . . . 30 - 40

Left to Right —
Canadian Shell (No. 9) Ht. 2" . . . . $40 - $50
Tassel. (No. 12) Ht. 2¼" . . . . 25 - 30

Left to Right —
Canadian Corn (No. 6) Ht. 3" .... $50 - $55
Butterfly & Tassel (No. 1) Ht. 3" .... 35 - 45
Swirl (No. 4) Ht. 2¾" .... 25 - 30

NOTE: To date the number 5 shaker has not been identified and we have not yet found an example of number 11 to photograph.

Left to Right —
Number Seven Design. (No. 7) Ht. 3¾" .... $40 - $45
Frame & Shell. (No. 8) Ht. 3¾" .... 35 - 45
Beaded Lattice & Frame (No. 10) Ht. 3¾" .... 40 - 45

DEPRESSION GLASS

Clear and coloured glassware made primarily during the Great Depression which began in 1929. This mass produced type of pressed glass was inexpensive to manufacture and available in a wide variety of designs. Some patterns made before and after the depression era are included in this category and "depression glass" is the term generally used to describe the many patterns and styles made from about 1925 to the late 1960's.

ADAM — GREEN

Ash Tray, 4¾"	. .	30.00	— 35.00
Bowls —			
7¾"	. . . . .	27.00	— 30.00
Cereal, 5¾"	. .	40.00	— 45.00
Covered, 9"	. .	95.00	— 115.00
Dessert, 4¾"	. .	18.00	— 20.00
Open, 9"	. . . .	50.00	— 55.00
Oval, 10"	. .	30.00	— 35.00
Butter Dish, covered	. . . . .		275.00
Cake Plate, ftd. 10"	25.00	— 30.00
Candlesticks, 4" pr.	100.00	— 110.00
Candy Jar, cvd. 2½"	115.00	— 125.00
Coaster, 3¼"	. .	20.00	— 25.00
Creamer	. . . . .	20.00	— 25.00
Sugar, cov.	. .	70.00	— 75.00
Sugar, open	. . . .		25.00
Cup	. . . . .	25.00	— 30.00
Saucer/Sherbet	7.00	— 10.00
Pitcher, 32 oz. 8"	45.00	— 50.00
Plates —			
Dinner, sq. 9"	25.00	— 30.00
Grill, 9"	. . . .	18.00	— 22.00
Salad, sq. 7¾"	. . . .		15.00
Sherbet, sq. 6"	7.00	— 10.00
Platter	. . . . .	25.00	— 27.00
Relish, divided, 8"	20.00	— 25.00
S & P Shakers, pr.	. . . .		130.00
Sherbet, 3"	. . . .	35.00	— 45.00
Tumblers —			
4½"	. . . . .	26.00	— 30.00
Iced Tea, 5½"	50.00	— 55.00
Vase, 7½"	. . . .		60.00

ADAM — PINK

Ash Tray, 4¾"	. .	35.00	— 40.00
Bowls —			
7¾"	. . . . .	22.00	— 25.00
Cereal, 5¾"	. .	50.00	— 55.00
Covered, 9"	. .	70.00	— 75.00
Dessert, 4¾"	. .	15.00	— 20.00
Open, 9"	. . . .	30.00	— 35.00
Oval, 10"	. .	30.00	— 35.00
Butter Dish, cvd.	90.00	— 100.00
Cake Plate, ftd. 10"	25.00	— 30.00
Candlesticks, 4" pr.	100.00	— 115.00
Candy Jar, cvd. 2½"	100.00	— 110.00
Coaster, 3¼"	. .	30.00	— 35.00
Creamer	. . . . .	18.00	— 20.00
Sugar, cvd.	. .	35.00	— 45.00
Sugar, open	. . . .		20.00
Cup	. . . .		25.00
Saucer/Sherbet	7.00	— 10.00
Pitchers —			
32 oz., 8"	. .	45.00	— 50.00
Round base, 32oz.	55.00	— 60.00
Plates —			
Dinner, sq. 9"	28.00	— 30.00
Grill, 9"	. . . .		24.00
Salad, sq. 7¾"	. . . .		16.00
Sherbet, sq. 6"	7.00	— 10.00
Platter	. . . . .	25.00	— 27.00
Relish, divided, 8"	20.00	— 22.00
S & P Shakers, pr.	65.00	— 75.00
Sherbet, 3"	. . . .	28.00	— 30.00
Tumblers —			
4½"	. . . . .	30.00	— 33.00
Iced Tea, 5½"	. . . . . .		75.00
Vase, 7½"	. . . .		200.00

AMERICAN SWEETHEART — MONAX

Bowls —

Berry, rd., 9"	60.00	—	65.00
Cereal, 6"	. . . .		15.00
Cream Soup, 4½"	65.00	—	70.00
Flat Soup, 9½"	65.00	—	70.00
Vegetable, oval	70.00	—	75.00
Creamer, ftd. . .	10.00	—	15.00
Sugar, ftd., cvd.			235.00
Sugar, ftd., open	8.00	—	10.00
Cup	10.00	—	13.00
Saucer	4.00	—	6.00

Plates —

Bread & Butter	5.00	—	7.00
Chop, 11" . .	15.00	—	17.00
Dinner, 9¾" . .	22.00	—	24.00
Luncheon, 9"	. . . .		15.00
Salad, 8"	8.00	—	12.00
Salver, 12"	. . . .		16.00
Platter, oval, 13"	70.00	—	75.00
S & P Shakers, ftd, pr	. . . . . .		260.00
Sherbet, ftd, 4¼"	19.00	—	22.00
Tid-bit, 2 tier,			
8" & 12"			75.00

AMERICAN SWEETHEART — PINK

Bowls —

Berry, flat, 3¾"	40. 00	—	45.00
Berry, rd., 9"	35.00	—	40.00
Cereal, 6" . .	13.00	—	17.00
Cream Soup, 4½"	45.00	—	50.00
Flat Soup, 9½"	45.00	—	50.00
Vegetable, oval,	50.00	—	55.00
Creamer, ftd. . .	15.00	—	20.00
Sugar, ftd. open	10.00	—	13.00
Cup	15.00	—	20.00
Saucer	4.00	—	6.00

Plates —

Bread & Butter	5.00	—	6.00
Dinner, 9¾" . .	25.00	—	35.00
Salad, 8"	12.00	—	14.00
Salver, 12" . .	20.00	—	22.00
Platter, oval, 13"	35.00	—	40.00
Pitcher, 60 oz. 7½"			500.00
S & P Shakers, ftd. pr			350.00

Sherbet —

Footed, 3¾" . .	18.00	—	20.00
Footed, 4¼" . .	14.00	—	18.00
Tid-bit, 2 tier,			
8" & 12"			75.00

Tumblers —

5 oz. 3½" . .	70.00	—	75.00
9 oz. 4¼" . .	65.00	—	70.00
10 oz. 4¾" . .	70.00	—	75.00

BLOCK OPTIC — GREEN

Bowls —
4¼"	. . . .		9.00
4½"	. . . . . 30.00	—	35.00
Berry, 8½"	. . 25.00	—	30.00
Cereal, 5¼"	. . 12.00	—	15.00
Salad, 7"	. . . . 25.00	—	30.00
Butter, cvd. 3 x 5	40.00	—	50.00
Candlesticks, pr.	100.00	—	120.00
Candy, cvd. 2¼"	50.00	—	55.00
Candy, cvd. 6¼"	55.00	—	60.00
Comport/Mayo, 4"	35.00	—	40.00
Creamer, all styles	15.00	—	17.00
Sugar, open	. . 10.00	—	13.00
Cup, all styles	. . . .		9.00
Saucer	. . . .		10.00

Goblets —
Cocktail, 4"	. . 40.00	—	45.00
Wine, 4½"	. . 40.00	—	45.00
9 oz., 5¾"	. . 25.00	—	30.00
Ice Bucket	. . . . 40.00	—	45.00
Ice/Butter Tub	. . 45.00	—	50.00
Mug	. . . . 40.00	—	45.00

Pitchers —
Bulbous, 54 oz.	75.00	—	80.00
54 oz., 8½"	. . 40.00	—	45.00
80 oz., 8"	. . 70.00	—	75.00

Plates —
Dinner, 9"	. . 20.00	—	25.00
Grill, 9"	. . . .		15.00
Luncheon, 8"	. . . .		7.00
Sandwich, 10¼"	25.00	—	30.00
Sherbet, 6"	. . 3.00	—	5.00

S & P Shakers —
Footed, pr.	. . 40.00	—	45.00
Squatty, pr.	. . 85.00	—	95.00
Sandwich Server	65.00	—	70.00

Sherbets —
Cone shape	. . 5.00	—	7.00
3¼"	. . . . . . 7.00	—	9.00
4¾"	. . . . . . 15.00	—	18.00

Tumblers —
3 oz. 2 5/8"	. . 20.00	—	25.00
Fl. 5 oz. 3½"	20.00	—	25.00
Fl. 9½ oz. 3¾"	15.00	—	18.00
Fl 10 oz. 5"	. . 20.00	—	22.00
Fl. 12 oz. 4 7/8"	25.00	—	30.00
Fl. 15 oz. 5¼"	40.00	—	45.00
Ftd. 3 oz. 3¼"	28.00	—	30.00
Ftd. 9 oz.	. . 20.00	—	22.00
Ftd. 10 oz. 6"	65.00	—	70.00
Tumble-up set	65.00	—	70.00
Vase, 5¾"	. . . .		225.00
Whiskey, 2 oz. 2¼"	30.00	—	35.00

BLOCK OPTIC — PINK

Bowls —
4¼"	. . . .		9.00
Berry, 8½"	. . 20.00	—	25.00
Cereal, 5¼"	. . 20.00	—	25.00
Candlesticks, pr.	90.00	—	100.00
Candy, cvd. 2¼"	55.00	—	60.00
Candy, cvd. 6¼"	110.00	—	125.00
Comport/Mayo, 4"	65.00	—	75.00
Creamer, all styles	15.00	—	17.00
Sugar, open	. . 12.00	—	14.00
Cup, all styles	. . . .		9.00
Saucer	. . . .		10.00

Goblets —
Cocktail, 4"	. . 40.00	—	45.00
Wine, 4½"	. . 40.00	—	45.00
9 oz., 5¾"	. . 30.00	—	35.00
Ice Bucket	. . . . 45.00	—	50.00
Ice/Butter Tub	. . 100.00	—	120.00

Pitchers —
54 oz., 8½"	. . 40.00	—	45.00
80 oz., 8"	. . 75.00	—	80.00

Plates —
Dinner, 9"	. . 25.00	—	30.00
Grill, 9"	. . . . 20.00	—	22.00
Luncheon, 8"	. . . .		7.00
Snadwich, 10¼"	20.00	—	25.00
Sherbet, 6"	. . 3.00	—	5.00

S & P Shakers,
Footed, pr.	. . 70.00	—	75.00
Sandwich Server	70.00	—	75.00

Sherbets —
3¼"	. . . . . . 10.00	—	12.00
4¾"	. . . . . . 15.00	—	18.00

Tumblers —
3 oz., 2 5/8"	. . 25.00	—	30.00
Fl. 5 oz. 3½"	25.00	—	30.00
Fl. 9½ oz. 3¾"	15.00	—	18.00
Fl. 10 oz. 5"	. . 15.00	—	20.00
Fl. 12 oz. 4 7/8"	20.00	—	25.00
Fl. 15 oz., 5¼"	40.00	—	45.00
Ftd., 3 oz., 3¼"	25.00	—	30.00
Ftd., 9 oz.	. . 15.00	—	20.00
Ftd., 10 oz. 6"	30.00	—	33.00
Whiskey, 1 oz., 1¾"	50.00	—	55.00
Whiskey, 2 oz., 2¼"	30.00	—	33.00

BUBBLE BLUE

Bowls —

Berry, 4"	10.00	—	15.00
Berry, 8 3/8"	16.00	—	20.00
Cereal, 5¼"	13.00	—	15.00
Flat Soup, 7 3/8"	14.00	—	16.00
Fruit, 4½"	10.00	—	13.00
Creamer	35.00	—	40.00
Sugar, open	20.00	—	22.00
Cup	3.00	—	5.00
Saucer	2.00	—	3.00

Plates —

Bread & Butter	3.50	—	5.00
Dinner, 9 3/8"	9.00	—	12.00
Grill, 9 3/8"	17.00	—	20.00
Platter, oval, 12"	16.00	—	18.00

BUBBLE — CRYSTAL

Bowls —

Berry, 4"			6.00
Berry, 8 3/8"			7.00
Cereal, 5¼"			5.00
Flat Soup, 7 3/8"			6.00
Fruit, 4½"	6.00	—	8.00
Candlesticks, pr.			18.00
Creamer	6.00	—	8.00
Sugar, open	6.00	—	8.00
Cup	3.00	—	5.00
Saucer	2.00	—	3.00
Lamp	50.00	—	55.00
Pitcher, ice lip, 64 oz	70.00	—	75.00

Plates —

Bread & Butter,	2.00	—	3.00
Dinner, 9 3/8"			6.00
Platter, oval, 12"	10.00	—	12.00

Stemware,—

Cocktail, 3½ oz			5.00
Cocktail, 4½ oz.			6.00
Goblet, 9 oz.			10.00
Goblet, 9½ oz.			10.00
Iced Tea, 14 oz.			10.00
Juice, 4 oz.			6.00
Juice, 5½ oz.			7.00
Sherbet, 6 oz.			5.00

BUBBLE — CRYSTAL

Tumblers —

Iced Tea, 12 oz, 4½"			9.00
Juice, 6 oz.			5.00
Lemonade, 16 oz.	12.00	—	15.00
Old Fashioned, 8 oz			9.00
Water, 9 oz.			7.00

BUBBLE — FOREST GREEN

Bowls —

Berry, 8 3/8"	10.00	—	15.00
Cereal, 5¼"	13.00	—	15.00
Fruit, 4½"	8.00	—	10.00
Candlesticks, pr.	30.00	—	35.00
Creamer	12.00	—	15.00
Sugar, open	12.00	—	16.00
Cup			7.00
Saucer	4.00	—	5.00

Plates —

Bread & Butter	3.50	—	5.00
Dinner, 9 3/8"	15.00	—	18.00

Stemware —

Cocktail, 3½ oz.			10.00
Cocktaile, 4½ oz.			10.00
Goblet, 9 oz.	15.00	—	18.00
Goblet, 9½ oz.	15.00	—	18.00
Iced Tea, 14 oz.	20.00	—	25.00
Juice, 4 oz.			11.50
Juice, 5½ oz.	13.00	—	15.00
Sherbet, 6 oz.			10.00

BUBBLE — RUBY RED

Bowls —

Berry, 8 3/8"	20.00	—	25.00
Fruit, 4½"	10.00	—	12.00
Cup			8.50
Saucer	4.00	—	5.00
Pitcher, ice lip, 64 oz.	60.00	—	65.00
Plate, dinner, 9 3/8"			12.00

Stemware —

Cocktail, 3½ oz.	10.00	—	12.00
Cocktail, 4½ oz.	10.00	—	12.00
Goblet, 9 oz.	15.00	—	18.00
Goblet, 9½ oz.	15.00	—	18.00
Juice, 4 oz.	12.00	—	15.00
Juice, 5½ oz.	13.00	—	15.00
Sherbet, 6 oz.	10.00	—	12.00
Tid-bit, 2 tier	40.00	—	45.00

Tumblers —

Iced Tea, 12 oz.	12.00	—	15.00
Juice, 6 oz.	10.00	—	12.00
Lemonade, 16 oz.	20.00	—	25.00
Old Fashioned,	20.00	—	25.00
Water, 9 oz.	10.00	—	12.00

CAMEO — GREEN

Bowls —

Berry, 8¼" . .	40.00	—	45.00
Cereal, 5½" . .	40.00	—	50.00
Console, 3 legs	75.00	—	85.00
Cream Soup, 4¾"	70.00	—	75.00
Rimmed Soup, 9"	50.00	—	55.00
Salad, 7¼" . .	50.00	—	55.00
Vegetable, oval	25.00	—	30.00
Butter Dish, cvd.	200.00	—	225.00
Cake Plate, 3 legs	25.00	—	30.00
Cake Plate, flat . .	100.00	—	115.00
Candlesticks, 4" pr.	120.00	—	150.00
Candy, cvd. 4" . .	70.00	—	80.00
CAndy, cvd. 6½"	. . . .		175.00
Comport/Mayo, 5"	30.00	—	35.00
Cookie, cvd.	65.00	—	70.00
Creamer, 3¼" . .	25.00	—	35.00
Sugar, open, 3¼"	20.00	—	30.00
Creamer, 4¼" . .	30.00	—	35.00
Sugar, open, 4¼"	30.00	—	35.00
Cup	15.00	—	25.00
Saucer/Sherbet	5.00	—	7.00
Decanter & Stopper	. . . .		150.00
Domino Tray with indent	. . . .		125.00

Goblets —

Water, 6" . .	60.00	—	70.00
Wine, 4"	60.00	—	75.00

Pitchers —

Juice, 36 oz. . .	60.00	—	70.00
Water, 56 oz.	60.00	—	70.00

CAMEO — GREEN

Plates —

Closed handles, 10½"	. . . .		15.00
Dinner, 9½" .	20.00	—	25.00
Grill, 10½" . .	10.00	—	15.00
Grill, c.h., 10½"	65.00	—	75.00
Luncheon, 8"	12.00	—	15.00
Sandwich, 10"	15.00	—	20.00
Sherbet, 6" . .	5.00	—	7.00
Square, 8½" . .	40.00	—	50.00
Platter, c.h., 12"	25.00	—	30.00
Relish, footed, divided, 7½" . .	30.00	—	35.00
S & P Shakers, pr.	75.00	—	85.00

Sherbets —

4 7/8"	35.00	—	50.00
Blown, 3 1/8"	15.00	—	20.00
Molded, 3 1/8"	15.00	—	20.00

Tumblers —

15 oz. 5¼" . .	75.00	—	85.00
Fl. 10 oz., 4¾"	40.00	—	45.00
Fl. 11 oz., 5"	30.00	—	35.00
Ftd. 9 oz. 5"	30.00	—	35.00
Ftd. 11 oz. 5¾"	65.00	—	75.00
Juice, 5 oz. 3¾"	30.00	—	35.00
Water, 9 oz. 4"	30.00	—	35.00

Vase —

Bulbous, 8" . .	30.00	—	40.00
Footed, 5¾" . .	175.00	—	200.00
Water Bottle, White- house vinegar, dark green.	25.00	—	30.00

CANADIAN SWIRL —
PLAIN

Bowls —
Fruit, 7½"	3.50
Nappy, 4½"	2.00
Soup, 7½"	3.00
Butter Dish, covered	12.00
Cream & Covered Sugar	12.00
Cup & Saucer	6.00

Pitchers —
20 oz.	5.00
60 oz.	8.00

Plates —
Bread & Butter, 6"	3.00
Dinner, 9¾"	5.00
Salad, 8"	4.00
S & P Shakers, pr.	5.00
Sherbet	2.00
Tumblers — 4" 5 oz.	4.00
9½ oz.	5.00

CANADIAN HIAWATHA —
CRYSTAL

Butter Dish, covered	15.00
Cream & Open Sugar	10.00
Plate	3.00
Sherbet	2.50

CANADIAN SAGUENAY —
CRYSTAL

Cream Soup/Nappy	3.00
Butter Dish, covered	12.00
Cream & Open Sugar	5.00
Cup & Saucer	5.00
Plates — Luncheon, 8"	4.00
Sherbet, 6"	2.00
S & P Shakers, Pr.	10.00
Sherbet	2.00
Tumblers — Juice, 5 oz.	9.00
Water, 9 oz.	9.00

CANADIAN SAGUENAY —
COLOURED

Cream Soup/Nappy	10.00
Butter Dish, covered	20.00
Cream & Open Sugar	10.00
Cup & Saucer	7.00
Plates — Luncheon, 8"	6.00
Sherbet, 6"	4.00
Sherbet	5.00
Tumblers — Juice, 5 oz.	9.00
Water, 9 oz.	9.00

CANADIAN SWIRL —
STIPPLED

Bowls —
Nappy, 4½"	3.00
Butter Dish, covered	15.00
Cream & Open Sugar	10.00
Pitcher, 20 oz.	7.00
Plate, Bread & Butter, 6"	3.00
S & P Shakers, Pr.	5.00
Sherbet	3.00

CHERRY BLOSSOM – GREEN

Bowls –

Berry, 4¾"	. .	20.00 —	22.00
Berry, 8½"	. .	50.00 —	55.00
Cereal, 5¾"	. .	35.00 —	40.00
Flat Soup, 7¾"		60.00 —	65.00
Fruit, 3 legs, 10½"		65.00 —	70.00
Handled, 9"	. .	30.00 —	35.00
Vegetable, oval		35.00 —	40.00
Butter Dish, cvd.		90.00 —	100.00
Cake Plate, 3 legs		30.00 —	35.00
Coaster	. . . . .	12.00 —	15.00
Creamer	. . . . .	20.00 —	25.00
Sugar, cvd.	. .	35.00 —	40.00
Sugar, open	. .	20.00 —	25.00
Cup	. . . .	20.00 —	25.00
Saucer	. . . .	5.00 —	6.00
Mug, 7 oz.	. . . .		225.00

Pitchers –

AOP rd/sc 36 oz	55.00 —	65.00
PAT fl. 42 oz.	55.00 —	65.00
PAT ftd. 36 oz.	55.00 —	65.00

Plates –

Dinner, 9"	. . . .	22.00 —	25.00
Grill, 10"	. .	80.00 —	85.00
Grill, 9"	. . . .	28.00 —	30.00
Salad, 7"	. . . .	19.00 —	22.00
Sherbet, 6"	. .	7.00 —	9.00

Platters –

Divided, 13 x 13		60.00 —	70.00
Oval, 11"	. .	30.00 —	35.00
Sherbet	. . . . .	20.00 —	22.00
Tray, 10½"	. . . .		25.00

Tumblers –

AOP, ftd, 4 oz.	25.00 —	35.00
AOP, rd. ft. 9 oz.	35.00 —	40.00
AOP, sc. ft. 8 oz.	35.00 —	40.00
PAT, fl., 4 oz.	30.00 —	35.00
PAT, fl., 9 oz.	25.00 —	30.00
PAT, fl. 12 oz.	75.00 —	80.00

CHERRY BLOSSOM – PINK

Bowls –

Berry, 4¾"	. .	16.00 —	20.00
Berry, 8½"	. .	50.00 —	55.00
Cereal, 5¾"	. .	35.00 —	40.00
Flat Soup, 7¾"		60.00 —	65.00
Fruit, 3 legs	. .	65.00 —	70.00
Handled, 9"	. .	30.00 —	35.00
Vegetable, oval		35.00 —	40.00
Butter Dish, cvd.		80.00 —	85.00
Cake Plate, 3 legs		30.00 —	35.00
Coaster	. . . . .	12.00 —	15.00
Creamer	. . . . .	20.00 —	25.00
Sugar, cvd.	. .	30.00 —	35.00
Sugar, open	. .	15.00 —	20.00
Cup	. . . .	20.00 —	25.00
Saucer	. . . .	5.00 —	6.00
Mug, 7 oz.	. . . .		240.00

Pitchers –

AOP rd/sc 36 oz.	50.00 —	55.00
PAT fl, 42 oz.	55.00 —	65.00
PAT ftd. 36 oz.	55.00 —	65.00

Plates –

Dinner, 9"	. .	20.00 —	22.00
Grill, 9"	. . . .	25.00 —	30.00
Salad, 7"	. . . .	18.00 —	22.00
Sherbet, 6"	. .	7.00 —	9.00

Platters –

Divided, 13 x 13		60.00 —	70.00
Oval, 11"	. . . .	30.00 —	35.00
Sherbet	. . . . .	16.00 —	20.00
Tray, 10½"	. . . .	25.00 —	30.00

Tumblers –

AOP, ft. 4 oz.	20.00 —	22.00
AOP, rd. ft. 9 oz.	32.00 —	35.00
AOP, sc. ft. 8 oz.	32.00 —	35.00
PAT, fl. 4 oz.	20.00 —	25.00
PAT, fl, 9 oz.	20.00 —	25.00
PAT, fl. 12 oz.	60.00 —	65.00

COLONIAL BLOCK – GREEN/PINK

Bowls —

4"	7.00	—	9.00
7"	20.00	—	22.00
Butter Dish, cvd.	50.00	—	60.00
Butter Tub	45.00	—	50.00
Candy Jar, cvd. . .	40.00	—	45.00
Creamer			15.00
Sugar, cvd.			27.00
Sugar, open			15.00
Goblet			15.00
Pitcher	45.00	—	50.00
Powder Jar, cvd.	20.00	—	22.00
Sherbet	10.00	—	12.00

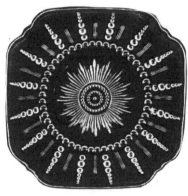

COLUMBIA – CRYSTAL

Bowls —

Cereal, 5" . .	15.00	—	18.00
Low Soup, 8"	15.00	—	18.00
Ruffled Edge	22.00	—	24.00
Salad, 8½" . .	15.00	—	18.00
Butter Dish, cvd.	22.00	—	24.00
Cup	5.00	—	7.00
Saucer	2.00	—	3.00

Plates —

Bread & Butter	3.00	—	4.00
Chop, 11". . . .	10.00	—	12.00
Luncheon, 9½"	7.00	—	10.00
Snack	45.00	—	50.00

Tumblers —

Juice, 4 oz. . .	20.00	—	24.00
Water, 9 oz. . .	18.00	—	20.00

COLONIAL KNIFE & FORK – GREEN

Bowls —

Berry, 4½" . .	12.00	—	15.00
Berry, 9"	25.00	—	30.00
Low Soup, 7"	55.00	—	60.00
Vegetable, oval	35.00	—	40.00
Butter Dish, cvd.	65.00	—	75.00
Creamer/Milk . .	25.00	—	30.00
Sugar, cvd. . .	75.00	—	80.00
Sugar, open . .	25.00	—	30.00
Cup			15.00
Saucer/Sherbet			6.00

Goblets —

Claret, 4 oz. . .	30.00	—	35.00
Cocktail, 3 oz.	30.00	—	35.00
Cordial, 1 oz.	35.00	—	40.00
Water, 8½ oz.	35.00	—	40.00
Wine, 2½ oz. . . .	30.00	—	35.00

Pitchers —

Milk/Creamer	25.00	—	30.00
54 oz., ...	60.00	—	65.00
68 oz.	80.00	—	85.00

Plates —

Dinner, 10" . .	70.00	—	75.00
Grill, 10"	25.00	—	30.00
Luncheon, . .	12.00	—	14.00
Sherbet/Saucer, 6"			6.00
Platter, oval, 12"	25.00	—	30.00
S & P Shakers, pr.			150.00
Sherbet, 3 3/8" . .	16.00	—	18.00
Spoon Holder/Celery			115.00

Tumblers —

11 oz, 5 1/8"	50.00	—	55.00
Ftd. 3 oz. . .	25.00	—	30.00
Ftd. 5 oz. . .	40.00	—	45.00
Ftd. 10 oz. . .	50.00	—	55.00
Iced Tea, 12 oz	55.00	—	60.00
Juice, 5 oz. . .	30.00	—	35.00
Water, 9 oz. . .	25.00	—	30.00
Whiskey, 1½ oz. . . .	15.00	—	18.00

ORIGINAL CORNFLOWER BY W. J. HUGHES

W.J. Hughes came to Canada from England in the early 1920's. He resided in Etobicoke (Toronto) and it was from his home that he first conducted his business of etching Cornflower on glass.

Hughes Cornflower is easily identified by its Trade Mark 12 Petals and a checkerboard centre. Very few exceptions to this rule.

Most of the glass on which he etched the Cornflower was imported from the U.S.A., plus some from Europe.

Some of the better known patterns he used were Candlewick — Imperial Glass Co.; Radiance — New Martinsville Glass Co.; Cambridge Glass; Heisey Glass; Fostoria Glass; Libbey Glass, just to name a few.

Brides of the 30's and 40's chose Cornflower as their crystal. Items to be found are in many shapes and sizes of stem-ware. Juice, water, iced tea tumblers. Salt and peppers; vases; candlesticks; bowls; butter dishes; salad servers; cream and sugars; pitchers, many sizes; swans; salad and sherbet plates, plus many, many more pieces.

It was produced in clear, referred to as crystal, but coloured glass was also used. Pink, green, blue, yellow and red. The coloured is not as abundant as the crystal and commands higher prices.

All Hughes Cornflower is very much in demand. It is also no longer produced.

By Edith Hacking
Director
The Canadian Depression Glass Club.

For those interested in Depression Glass, the Canadain Depression Glass Club issues an interesting newsletter ten times a year. For further information contact — Edith Hacking, P.O. Box 104, 3353 The Credit Woodlands, Mississauga, Ontario, L5C 2K1. Enclose a self-addressed stamped envelope.

CORNFLOWER GOBLET.
Pink, etched by Hughes of
Toronto. Maker of blank
not known.
Ht. 7" $25.00

CORNFLOWER VASE. Ht. 10¾"
Blank possibly by Fostoria Glass
Co., 1940's. $60.00

CORNFLOWER DECANTER.
Ht. 8¾" Maker of blank not
known. Original stopper.
Mint $75.00

CORNFLOWER BATTER PITCHER.
Ht. 5½" Blank, Radiant pattern by
New Martinsville Glass Co.
Mint. $85.00

CUBE — PINK

Bowls —

Deep, 4½" . .	6.00	—	8.00
Dessert, 4½" . .	6.00	—	8.00
Salad, 6½" . .	10.00	—	12.00
Butter Dish, cvd.	60.00	—	65.00
Candy, cvd. 6½"	30.00	—	35.00
Coaster, 3¼"	6.00	—	8.00
Creamer, 2 5/8" . .	3.00	—	5.00
Sugar, open, . .	3.00	—	5.00
Creamer, 3½" . .	7.00	—	9.00
Sugar, cvd. 3"	20.00	—	25.00
Sugar, open, 3"	10.00	—	12.00
Cup	7.00	—	9.00
Saucer	3.00	—	4.00
Plates —			
Luncheon, 8"	6.00	—	7.00
Sherbet, 6" . .	3.00	—	4.00
Powder Jar, cvd.	25.00	—	30.00
S & P Shakers, pr.	40.00	—	45.00
Sherbet, ftd.	6.00	—	8.00
Tumbler, 9 oz. 4"	65.00	—	70.00

CUBE — GREEN

Bowls —

Dessert, 4½" . .	7.00	—	9.00
Salad, 6½" . .	15.00	—	17.00
Butter Dish, cvd.	60.00	—	65.00
Candy, cvd. 6½"	35.00	—	40.00
Coaster, 3¼" . .	7.00	—	9.00
Creamer, 3½" . .	10.00	—	12.00
Sugar, cvd. 3"	20.00	—	25.00
Sugar, open 3"	10.00	—	12.00
Cup	10.00	—	12.00
Saucer	3.00	—	4.00
Plates —			
Luncheon, 8"	7.00	—	8.00
Sherbet, 6" . .	4.00	—	5.00
Powder Jar, cvd.	25.00	—	30.00
S & P Shakers, pr.	40.00	—	45.00
Sherbet, ftd.	9.00	—	12.00
Tumbler, 9 oz. 4"	70.00	—	75.00

DOGWOOD — PINK

Bowls —

Berry, 8½" . .	50.00	—	60.00
Cereal, 5½" . .	25.00	—	30.00
Creamer —			
Thin, flat, 2½"	20.00	—	25.00
Sugar —			
Thin, flat, 2½..	20.00	—	25.00
Creamer —			
Thick, ftd. 3¼" .	20.00	—	25.00
Sugar —			
Thick, ftd. 3¼"	20.00	—	25.00
Cup, thick/thin . .	13.00	—	18.00
Saucer			7.00
Pitcher — American Sweetheart			
style, 80 oz. 8"	200.00	—	210.00
Plates —			
Bread & Butter	8.00	—	10.00
Dinner, 9¼" . .	25.00	—	30.00
Grill, 10½" . .	20.00	—	24.00
Luncheon, 8"	8.00	—	10.00
Salver, 12" . .	25.00	—	30.00
Sherbet, low, ftd.	25.00	—	30.00

DOGWOOD — PINK

Tumblers — Decorated —			
10 oz. 4"	40.00	—	45.00
11 oz. 4¾" . .	50.00	—	55.00
12 oz. 5"	60.00	—	70.00

DORIC – GREEN

Bowls —

Berry, 4½"	. .	8.00	— 10.00
Berry, 8¼"	. .	20.00	— 22.00
Handled, 9"	. .	20.00	— 22.00
Vegetable, oval		30.00	— 35.00
Butter Dish, cvd.		100.00	— 125.00
Cake Plate, 3 legs		25.00	— 30.00
Candy, cvd. 8"	. .	40.00	— 45.00
Candy, 3 part	. .	10.00	— 15.00
Coaster, 3"	. . . .	18.00	— 20.00
Creamer, 4"	. . . .	15.00	— 20.00
Sugar, cvd.	. .	40.00	— 45.00
Cup	. . . .	10.00	— 12.00
Saucer	. . . .		5.00

Pitcher —

Flat, 36 oz., 6"		40.00	— 45.00

Plates —

Dinner, 9"	. .	15.00	— 18.00
Grill, 9"	. . . .	18.00	— 22.00
Salad, 7"	. . . .	18.00	— 22.00
Sherbet, 6"	. .	5.00	— 6.00
Platter, oval, 12"		25.00	— 30.00
Relish Tray, 4 x 4		10.00	— 12.00
Relish Tray, 4 x 8		14.00	— 18.00

S & P Shakers —

New tops	. . . .	35.00	— 40.00
Old tops	. . . .	45.00	— 50.00
Sherbet, ftd.	. . . .		17.00
Tray, handled, 10"		18.00	— 22.00
Tray, serving, 8 x 8		20.00	— 22.00

DORIC – PINK

Bowls —

Berry, 4½"	. .	8.00	— 10.00
Berry, 8¼"	. .	20.00	— 22.00
Handled, 9"	. .	20.00	— 22.00
Vegetable, oval		22.00	— 25.00
Butter Dish, cvd.		75.00	— 85.00
Cake Plate, 3 legs		25.00	— 30.00
Candy, cvd. 8"	. .	38.00	— 42.00
Candy, 3 part	. .	9.00	— 13.00
Coaster, 3"	. . . .	15.00	— 20.00
Creamer, 4"	. . . .	12.00	— 18.00
Sugar, cvd.	. .	25.00	— 30.00
Cup	. . . .	8.00	— 10.00
Saucer	. . . .		5.00

Pitcher —

Flat, 36 oz. 6"		40.00	— 45.00

Plates —

Dinner, 9"	. .	13.00	— 16.00
Grill, 9"	. . . . .	13.00	— 16.00
Salad, 7"	. . . .	18.00	— 20.00
Sherbet, 6"	. .	4.00	— 5.00
Platter, oval, 12"		22.00	— 26.00
Relish tray, 4 x 4		10.00	— 12.00
Relish Tray, 4 x 8		12.00	— 15.00

S & P Shakers —

New tops	. . . .	30.00	— 35.00
Old tops	. . . .	40.00	— 45.00
Sherbet, ftd.	. . . .		15.00
Tray, handled, 10"		15.00	— 20.00
Tray, serving, 8 x 8		20.00	— 22.00

Tumblers —

9 oz. 4½"	. .	45.00	— 50.00
Ftd. 10 oz. 4"		45.00	— 50.00
Ftd. 12 oz. 5"		60.00	— 65.00

Not illustrated —
FIRE-KING OVEN GLASS —
BLUE

Bakers —

Individual, 6 oz.	5.00	—	6.00
Round, 1 pt. . .	6.00	—	8.00
Round, 1 qt. . .	8.00	—	10.00
Round, 1½ qt.	10.00	—	15.00
Round, 2 qt. . .	15.00	—	18.00
Square, 4½ x 5	6.00	—	8.00

Bowls —

Cereal/Deep Dish Pie Plate, 5 3/8"	18.00	—	20.00
Individual Pie Plate, 4 3/8" . .	15.00	—	18.00
Measuring, 16 oz.	25.00	—	30.00

Cake Pan —

Deep, 8¾" . .	25.00	—	30.00

Casseroles —

Individual, 10 oz.	15.00	—	18.00
1 pt. knob handle cover	. .		18.00
1 qt. knob handle cover	. .		17.00
1½ qt. knob handle cover	. .		25.00
2 qt. knob handle cover	. .		25.00
1 qt. pie plate cover	. . . .		23.00
1½ qt. pie plate cover	. . . .		23.00
2 qt. pie plate cover	. . . . .		28.00

Custard Cup/Baker —

5 oz.	4.00	—	6.00
6 oz.	4.00	—	6.00

Loaf Pan —

Deep, 9 1/8" x 5 1/8"	23.00

Measuring Cups —

8 oz. 1 spout . .	20.00	—	25.00
8 oz. 3 spout . .	20.00	—	25.00
Mug, 7 oz.	25.00	—	30.00
Percolator Top, 2 1/8"	5.00	—	7.00

Pie Plates —

8 3/8"	10.00	—	12.00
9"	10.00	—	12.00
9 5/8"	10.00	—	14.00
Juice Saver, 10½"	80.00	—	85.00

Refrigerator Jars, cvd. —

4½" x 5"	15.00	—	18.00
5 1/8" x 9 1/8"	40.00	—	45.00

Roasters —

8¾"	40.00	—	50.00
10 3/8"	80.00	—	85.00

Table Server (Hot Plate) tab handles	20.00	—	25.00

Utility Bowls —

1 qt. 6 7/8" . .	14.00	—	16.00
1½ qt. 8 3/8"	20.00	—	22.00
10 1/8"	20.00	—	22.00

Utility Pans —

2 qt. 8 1/8 x 12½	35.00	—	40.00
10½ x 2 deep	25.00	—	30.00

Not illustrated —
FIRE-KING OVEN WARE -
TURQUOISE BLUE –

Ash Trays —

3½"	9.00
4 5/8"	10.00
5¾"	15.00

Bowls —

Batter, with spout	50.00	—	55.00
Berry, 4¼" . .	6.00	—	8.00
Cereal, 5" . .	8.00	—	10.00
Soup/Salad, 6½"	15.00	—	18.00
Vegetable, 8"	15.00	—	18.00
Creamer	6.00	—	8.00
Sugar, open . .	6.00	—	8.00
Cup	4.00	—	5.00
Saucer	1.00	—	2.00

Mixing Bowls —

Round, 1 qt . .	10.00	—	15.00
Round, 2 qt. . .	8.00	—	12.00
Round, 3 qt. . .	10.00	—	15.00
Round, 4 qt. . .	12.00	—	17.00
Teardrop, 1 pt.	10.00	—	15.00
Teardrop, 1 qt.	12.00	—	17.00
Teardrop, 2 qt.	17.00	—	20.00
Teardrop, 3 qt.	20.00	—	25.00
Mug, 8 oz.	10.00	—	12.00

Plates —

Egg, 9¾"	12.00	—	17.00
6 1/8"	10.00	—	12.00
7"	10.00	—	12.00
9"	8.00	—	10.00
9" with indent	8.00	—	10.00
10"	25.00	—	30.00
Relish, 3 part, 11"	10.00	—	15.00

164

FLORAGOLD — IRIDESCENT

Ash Tray/Coaster, 4"	8.00	—	10.00
Bowls —			
Cereal, rd. 5½"	35.00	—	40.00
Fruit,ruffled,5½"	10.00	—	12.00
Fruit,ruffled,12"	10.00	—	15.00
Ruffled, 9½"	10.00	—	15.00
Salad, deep, 9½"	40.00	—	45.00
Square, 4½" . .	7.00	—	9.00
Square, 8½" . .	18.00	—	20.00
Butter Dish —			
Oblong, cvd. . .	30.00	—	35.00
Round, cvd. 6¼"	50.00	—	55.00
Candlesticks, pr.	50.00	—	60.00
Candy, handled . .	12.00	—	15.00
Candy/Cheese, cvd.	55.00	—	65.00
Candy, 4 feet, 5¼"	8.00	—	10.00
Creamer	10.00	—	12.00
Sugar, cvd. . .	25.00	—	30.00
Sugar, open . .	8.00	—	10.00
Cup	6.00	—	8.00
Saucer, no ring	9.00	—	11.00
Pitcher, 64 oz. . .	35.00	—	40.00
Plates —			
Dinner, 8¼" . .	35.00	—	45.00
Sherbet, 5¼"	12.00	—	15.00
Platter, 11¼" . .	20.00	—	25.00
S & P Shakers, pr.	60.00	—	65.00
Sherbet, low, ftd.	18.00	—	22.00

FLORAGOLD — IRIDESCENT

Tray —			
13½" no indent	25.00	—	30.00
13½" indent . .	50.00	—	55.00
Tumblers —			
Footed, 10 oz.	20.00	—	25.00
Footed, 11 oz.	20.00	—	25.00
Footed, 15 oz.	80.00	—	90.00

AOP	. .	All over pattern
c.h.	. .	closed handles
cov'd.	. .	covered
c.s.	. .	cone shape
dec.	. .	decorated
fl.	. . . .	flat
ftd.	. .	footed
h.	. . . .	handled
n.t.	. .	new tops
ob.	. .	oblong
o.h.	. .	open handles
op.	. .	open
o.t.	. .	original tops
PAT	. .	Pattern at top
rd.	. . . .	round
sc.	. . . .	scalloped
sq.	. . . .	square
und.	. .	undecorated

FLORAL — GREEN

Bowls —

Berry, 4"	18.00	—	22.00
Salad, 7½" . .	22.00	—	24.00
Vegetable, cvd.	55.00	—	60.00
Vegetable, op.	20.00	—	22.00
Butter Dish, cvd.	100.00	—	110.00
Candlesticks, 4" pr.	80.00	—	90.00
Candy, cvd.	40.00	—	45.00
Coaster, 3¼" . .	10.00	—	15.00
Creamer	14.00	—	19.00
Sugar, cvd. . .	30.00	—	35.00
Sugar, open . .	12.00	—	15.00
Cup	15.00	—	17.00
Saucer	13.00	—	15.00

Pitcher, —

Cone shape, 32 oz.	40.00	—	45.00
Lemonade, 48oz.			245.00

Plates —

Dinner, 9" . .	18.00	—	22.00
Salad, 8"	13.00	—	15.00
Sherbet, 6" . .	7.00	—	9.00
Platter, oval, 10¾"	18.00	—	22.00
Refrigerator Dish, covered, 5 x 5	75.00	—	80.00
Relish, 2 part . .	16.00	—	20.00
S & P Shakers, ftd	60.00	—	65.00
Sherbet	18.00	—	22.00
Tray, sq. 6 x 6 . .	20.00	—	25.00

Tumblers —

Juice, ftd. 5 oz.	25.00	—	30.00
Lemonade, ftd.	50.00	—	55.00
Water, ftd. 7 oz.	27.00	—	32.00

FLORAL — PINK

Bowls —

Berry, 4"	17.00	—	20.00
Salad, 7½" . .	15.00	—	20.00
Vegetable, cvd.	48.00	—	55.00
Vegetable, op.	18.00	—	20.00
Butter Dish, cvd.	90.00	—	100.00
Candlesticks, 4" pr	70.00	—	80.00
Candy, cvd.	40.00	—	45.00
Coaster, 3¼" . .	14.00	—	18.00
Creamer	14.00	—	18.00
Sugar, cvd. . .	20.00	—	25.00
Sugar, open . .	10.00	—	12.00
Cup	12.00	—	14.00
Saucer	6.00	—	8.00

Pitcher —

Cone shape, 32 oz.	35.00	—	40.00
Lemonade, 48 oz.			295.00

Plates —

Dinner, 9" . .	15.00	—	20.00
Salad, 8"	10.00	—	12.00
Sherbet, 6" . .	6.00	—	8.00
Platter, oval, 10¾"	20.00	—	22.00
Relish, 2 part . .	18.00	—	22.00
S & P Shakers, fl.	55.00	—	60.00
S & P Shakers, ftd.	50.00	—	60.00
Sherbet	14.00	—	17.00
Tray, sq. 6 x 6 . .	14.00	—	18.00

Tumblers —

Juice, ftd. 5 oz.	20.00	—	24.00
Lemonade, ftd.	45.00	—	50.00
Water, ftd. 7 oz.	20.00	—	24.00

FLORENTINE NO. 2 — GREEN

Ash Tray/ Coaster —			
3¾"	25.00	—	30.00
5½"	25.00	—	30.00
Bowls —			
5½"	40.00	—	45.00
Berry, 4½"	12.00	—	15.00
Berry, 8"	20.00	—	25.00
Cereal, 6"	30.00	—	35.00
Cream Soup, 4¾"	16.00	—	20.00
Flat, 9"	25.00	—	30.00
Vegetable, cvd.	60.00	—	65.00
Butter Dish, cvd.	120.00	—	135.00
Candlesticks, 2¾"	55.00	—	60.00
Candy, cvd.	100.00	—	125.00
Comport, reffled	25.00	—	30.00
Creamer	10.00	—	12.00
Sugar, cvd.	25.00	—	30.00
Sugar, open	10.00	—	12.00
Cup	8.00	—	10.00
Saucer			5.00
Custard Cup/Jello	75.00	—	80.00
Custard/Jello &			
6¼" plate	90.00	—	105.00
Pitchers —			
48 oz. 7½"	60.00	—	70.00
76 oz. 8¼"	100.00	—	120.00
C.S. ftd. 28 oz.	30.00	—	40.00
Plates —			
Dinner, 10"	17.00	—	20.00
Grill, 10¼"	15.00	—	17.00
Salad, 8½"	10.00	—	12.00
Sherbet, 6"	4.00	—	6.00
With indent 6¼"			15.00
Platter, oval 11"	15.00	—	20.00
Relish Dish, 10"	20.00	—	25.00
S & P Shakers, pr.	50.00	—	60.00
Sherbet, ftd.	10.00	—	12.00
Tumblers —			
Ftd. 5 oz. 3¼"	15.00	—	17.00
Ftd. 5 oz. 4"	16.00	—	18.00
Ftd. 9 oz. 4½"	25.00	—	30.00
Iced Tea, 12 oz	35.00	—	45.00
Juice, 5 oz.	15.00	—	17.00
Vase/Parfait, 6"	35.00	—	45.00

FLORENTINE NO. 2 — YELLOW

Ash Tray/Coaster —			
5½"	40.00	—	45.00
Bowls —			
5½"	45.00	—	50.00
Berry, 4½"	20.00	—	24.00
Berry, 8"	30.00	—	35.00
Cereal, 6"	40.00	—	45.00
Cream Soup, 4¾"	22.00	—	27.00
Vegetable, cvd.	65.00	—	75.00
Butter Dish, cvd.	175.00	—	200.00
Candlesticks, 2¾"	70.00	—	75.00
Candy, cvd.	175.00	—	200.00
Creamer	12.00	—	15.00
Sugar, cvd	40.00	—	45.00
Sugar, open	12.00	—	15.00
Cup	12.00	—	14.00
Saucer	4.00	—	6.00
Custard Cup/Jellow			125.00
Custard/Jello &			
6¼" plate			150.00
Gravy Boat	60.00	—	65.00
Platter	45.00	—	50.00
Pitchers —			
48 oz. 7½"			235.00
C.S. ftd. 24 oz.	125.00	—	150.00
C.S. ftd. 28 oz.	35.00	—	40.00
Plates —			
Dinner, 10"	18.00	—	24.00
Grill, 10¼"	12.00	—	15.00
Salad, 8½"	10.00	—	12.00
Sherbet, 6"	5.00	—	7.00
With indent 6¼"			25.00
Platter, oval, 11"	18.00	—	24.00
Relish Dish, 10"	30.00	—	35.00
S & P Shakers, pr.	50.00	—	60.00
Sherbet, ftd.	10.00	—	13.00
Tray, condiment			95.00
Tumblers —			
Ftd. 5 oz. 4"	18.00	—	22.00
Ftd. 9 oz. 4½"	30.00	—	45.00
Iced Tea, 12 oz.	50.00	—	55.00
Juice, 5 oz.	24.00	—	27.00
Vase/Parfait, 6"	75.00	—	80.00

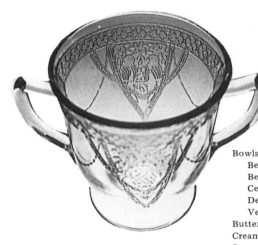

GEORGIAN LOVEBIRDS – GREEN

Bowls —
Berry, 4½"	, .	9.00 —	11.00
Berry, 7½"	. .	70.00 —	75.00
Cereal, 5¾"	. .	20.00 —	22.00
Deep, 6½"	. .	80.00 —	85.00
Vegetable,9"	. .	67.00 —	75.00
Butter Dish, cvd..	.	100.00 —	110.00
Creamer, ftd. 4"		15.00 —	18.00
Sugar, open	. . . .	12.00 —	14.00
Cup	. . . .		11.00
Saucer	. . . .	3.00 —	4.00
Hot Plate, 5"	. .	50.00 —	60.00

Plates —
Centre design, 9¼"	25.00 —	28.00
Dinner, 9¼"	. .	28.00 —	33.00
Luncheon, 8".	.	8.00 —	10.00
Sherbet, 6"	. .	5.00 —	7.00
Platter, c.h. 11½"	65.00 —	75.00
Sherbet	. . . . . .	12.00 —	16.00

Tumblers —
Flat, 9 oz. 4"	60.00 —	65.00
Flat, 12 oz. 5¼"	80.00 —	90.00

HOLIDAY – PINK

Bowls —
Berry, 5 1/8"		11.00 —	15.00
Berry, 8½"	. .	25.00 —	30.00
Console, 10¾"		100.00 —	110.00
Soup, 7¾"	. .	50.00 —	55.00
Vegetable, oval		20.00 —	25.00
Butter Dish, cvd.		50.00 —	60.00
Cake Plate, 3 legs		95.00 —	105.00
Candlesticks, 3" pr.	100.00 —	110.00
Creamer, ftd.	. .	10.00 —	12.00
Sugar, cvd.	. .	25.00 —	30.00
Sugar, open	. .	10.00 —	12.00
Cup, 3 sizes	. . . .	7.00 —	9.00
Saucer, plain/rayed	. .	6.00 —	7.50

Pitchers —
52 oz. 6 ¾"	. .	35.00 —	40.00
Milk, 16 oz. 4¾"	60.00 —	75.00

Plates —
Chop, 13¾"	. .	100.00 —	110.00
Dinner, 9"	. . .	15.00 —	20.00
Sherbet, 6"	. .	5.00 —	6.00
Platter, oval, 11 3/8"	22.00 —	25.00
Sandwich tray,10½"	18.00 —	22.00
Sherbet	. . . . . .	7.00 —	10.00

Tumblers —
Flat, 10 oz. 4"	22.00 —	27.00
Ftd. 5 oz. 4"	40.00 —	45.00
Ftd. 6"	. . . .	110.00 —	130.00

HOMESPUN —
CRYSTAL/PINK

Ash Tray / Coaster	8.00	—	9.00
Bowls —			
Berry, 8¼" . .	20.00	—	25.00
Cereal, 5" . .	20.00	—	25.00
Closed handles,4½"8.00		—	9.00
Butter Dish, cvd.	60.00	—	75.00
Creamer, ftd. . .	10.00	—	12.00
Sugar, open . .	10.00	—	12.00
Cup	8.00	—	10.00
Saucer	4.00	—	5.00
Plates —			
Dinner, 9¼" . .	18.00	—	22.00
Sherbet, 6" . .	4.00	—	6.00
Platter, c.h. 13" . .	18.00	—	20.00
Sherbet	15.00	—	22.00
Tumblers —			
Footed, 5 oz. 4"	8.00	—	10.00
Footed, 15 oz.	34.00	—	36.00
Iced Tea, 13 oz.	30.00	—	35.00
Straight, 9 oz.	22.00	—	24.00
Water, 9 oz. . .	22.00	—	24.00

HOMESPUN —
CHILD'S TEA SET
CRYSTAL

Set, 12 pieces, . .			
boxed	135.00	—	150.00
Cup	20.00	—	22.00
Saucer	6.00	—	8.00
Plate	8.00	—	9.00

HOMESPUN —
CHILD'S TEA SET
PINK

Set, 14 pieces,			
boxed	325.00	—	350.00
Cup	35.00	—	38.00
Saucer	9.00	—	11.00
Plate	12.00	—	15.00
Tea Pot	45.00	—	50.00
Tea Pot Lid	55.00	—	60.00

IRIS — CRYSTAL

Bowls —

Berry, beaded, 4½"	40.00	—	45.00
Cereal, 5" ..	50.00	—	60.00
Fruit, ruffled, 11½"	15.00	—	20.00
Fruit, straight, 11"	55.00	—	65.00
Salad, ruffled, 9½"	15.00	—	18.00
Sauce, ruffled, 5"	10.00	—	15.00
Soup, 7½" ..	120.00	—	130.00
Butter Dish, cvd.	50.00	—	60.00
Candlesticks, pr.	35.00	—	40.00
Candy, cvd.	135.00	—	150.00
Creamer, ftd....	10.00	—	14.00
Sugar, cvd. ..	20.00	—	25.00
Sugar, open ..	10.00	—	15.00
Cup	14.00	—	16.00
Saucer	9.00	—	11.00
Demi Tasse	35.00	—	40.00
Saucer	100.00	—	125.00
Fruit/nut set	50.00	—	55.00

Goblets —

4 oz. 5¾" ..	25.00	—	30.00
8 oz. 5¾" ..	25.00	—	30.00
Cocktail, 4 oz.	25.00	—	30.00
Wine, 3 oz. ..	20.00	—	25.00
Lamp Shade, 11½"	50.00	─·	55.00
Pitcher, ftd. 9½"	40.00	—	45.00

Plates —

Dinner, 9" ..	55.00	—	60.00
Luncheon, 8"	65.00	—	70.00
Salver/ Sandwich, 11¾"	25.00	—	30.00
Sherbet, 5½"	12.00	—	15.00
Sherbet, ftd. 2¼"	25.00	—	30.00
Sherbet, ftd. 4" ..	20.00	—	22.00

Tumblers —

Footed, 6" ..	18.00	—	25.00
Footed, 6½" ..	30.00	—	35.00
Vase, 9"	27.00	—	32.00

IRIS — MARIGOLD

Bowls —

Berry, beaded, 4½"	10.00	—	15.00
Berry, beaded, 8"	18.00	—	20.00
Fruit, ruffled, 11½"	15.00	—	20.00
Salad, ruffled, 9½"	15.00	—	18.00
Sauce, ruffled, 5"	25.00	—	30.00
Soup, 7½" ..	50.00	—	55.00
Butter Dish, cvd.	45.00	—	55.00
Candlesticks, pr.	45.00	—	50.00
Creamer, ftd. ..	10.00	—	15.00
Sugar, cvd. ..	20.00	—	25.00
Sugar, open ..	10.00	—	15.00
Cup	12.00	—	14.00
Saucer	8.00	—	10.00
Fruit/nut set	55.00	—	60.00
Pitcher, ftd. 9½"	45.00	—	50.00

Plates

Dinner, 9" ..	40.00	—	50.00
Salver/ Sandwich, 11¾"	25.00	—	30.00
Sherbet, 5½"	12.00	—	15.00
Sherbet, ftd. 2¼"	15.00	—	20.00

Tumbler —

Footed, 6" ..	18.00	—	25.00
Vase, 9"	25.00	—	30.00

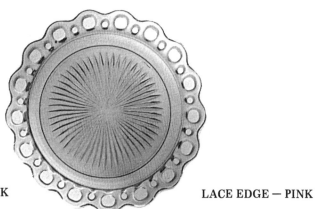

LACE EDGE — PINK

Bowls —
Cereal, 6 3/8"	18.00	—	22.00
Frosted, 3 legs	175.00	—	225.00
Plain/Ribbed,9½"	22.00	—	25.00
Salad,ribbed,7¾"	50.00	—	55.00

Butter Dish/
Bon-Bon, cvd.	70.00	—	80.00

Candlesticks,
Frosted, pr . .	50.00	—	55.00
Candy, cvd.	55.00	—	60.00

Comports —
7"	25.00	—	30.00
Ftd. cvd. 7" . .	60.00	—	75.00
Cookie Jar, cvd. . .	70.00	—	75.00
Creamer	25.00	—	30.00
Sugar, open . .	25.00	—	30.00
Cup, etched	17.00	—	20.00
Cup, plain	25.00	—	30.00
Saucer	10.00	—	15.00
Flower Bowl	28.00	—	30.00

Flower Bowl with
crystal frog . .	30.00	—	35.00

LACE EDGE — PINK

Plates —
Dinner, 8¾" . .	25.00	—	30.00
Grill, 10½" . .	20.00	—	25.00
Luncheon, 8¾"	18.00	—	22.00
Salad, 8¼" . .	20.00	—	22.00
Solid Lace, 13"	30.00	—	35.00

Platters —
12¾"	28.00	—	35.00
12¾" 5 part . .	28.00	—	35.00

Relish —
7½" 3 part . .	65.00	—	75.00
10½" 3 part . .	25.00	—	30.00
13" 4 part . .	30.00	—	35.00
Sherbet, ftd.	90.00	—	100.00

Tumblers —
Flat, 5 oz. . .	25.00	—	30.00
Flat, 9 oz. . .	17.00	—	20.00
Ftd. 10½" . .	65.00	—	70.00
Vase, frosted, 7"	65.00	—	75.00

LORAIN — YELLOW

Bowls —
Cereal, 6" . .	60.00	—	70.00
Salad, 7¼" . , .	60.00	—	70.00
Vegetable, oval	50.00	—	60.00
Creamer, ftd. . .	25.00	—	30.00
Sugar, open . .	25.00	—	30.00
Cup	15.00	—	20.00
Saucer	6.00	—	8.00

Plates —
Dinner, 10¼" .	60.00	—	70.00
Luncheon, 8 3/8"	30.00	—	35.00
Salad, 7¾" . .	15.00	—	20.00
Sherbet, 5½" . .	12.00	—	14.00
Platter, 11½" . .	45.00	—	50.00
Relish, 4 part, 8"	45.00	—	50.00
Sherbet, ftd.	35.00	—	40.00

Tumbler —
Ftd, 9 oz. 4¾"	30.00	—	35.00

MADRID — AMBER

Bowls —

Berry, 9 3/8"	25.00	—	30.00
Console, low, 11"	19.00	—	24.00
Cream soup, 4¾"	17.00	—	20.00
Salad, 8"	18.00	—	25.00
Salad, deep, 9½"	30.00	—	35.00
Sauce, 5" . .	7.00	—	10.00
Soup, 7"	15.00	—	20.00
Vegetable, oval	20.00	—	25.00
Butter Dish, cvd.	75.00	—	85.00
Candlesticks, pr.	30.00	—	35.00
Cookie Jar, cvd. . .	50.00	—	55.00
Creamer, ftd. . .	12.00	—	15.00
Sugar, open . .	10.00	—	12.00
Cup	8.00	—	10.00
Saucer	5.00	—	7.00
Jam Dish, 7" . .	25.00	—	30.00
Jello Mould, 2 1/8"	13.00	—	18.00

Pitchers —

80 oz. 8½" . .	55.00	—	65.00
Ice Lip, 80 oz.	55.00	—	65.00
Juice, 36 oz. . . .	40.00	—	45.00
Square, 60 oz.	45.00	—	55.00

MADRID — AMBER

Plates —

Cake, round, 11¼	20.00	—	25.00
Dinner, 10½"	35.00	—	40.00
Grill, 10½" . .	12.00	—	14.00
Luncheon, 8 7/8	11.00	—	14.00
Relish, 10¼"	14.00	—	17.00
Salad, 7½"	13.00	—	15.00
Sherbet, 6" . .	4.00	—	6.00
Platter, oval, 11½"	15.00	—	19.00
S & P Shakers, fl.	60.00	—	65.00
S & P Shakers, ftd.	85.00	—	90.00
Sherbet, two styles	10.00	—	12.00

Tumblers —

9 oz. 4¼" . .	15.00	—	20.00
12 oz. 5½" . .	24.00	—	27.00
Footed, 5 oz. 4"	28.00	—	30.00
Footed, 10 oz.	28.00	—	30.00

172

MANHATTAN — CRYSTAL

Ash Trays —
Round, 4" . .	15.00	—	17.00
Square, 4½" . .	14.00	—	19.00

Bowls —
Berry, h., 5 3/8"	17.00	—	20.00
Bery, 7½" . .	16.00	—	18.00
Cereal, 5½" . .	35.00	—	40.00
Closed handles	20.00	—	25.00
Fruit, 9½" . .	25.00	—	35.00
Salad, 9"	25.00	—	30.00
Sauce, h., 4½"	10.00	—	13.00
Candlesticks, sq. pr.	18.00	—	20.00
Candy, cvd.	40.00	—	45.00
Coaster, 3½" . .	12.00	—	16.00
Comport, 5¾" . .	30.00	—	35.00
Creamer	12.00	—	14.00
Sugar, open . .	12.00	—	14.00
Cup	20.00	—	24.00
Saucer/Sherbet	8.00	—	10.00

Pitchers —
24 oz.	35.00	—	40.00
Tilt, 80 oz. . .	45.00	—	50.00

Plates —
Dinner, 10¼"	19.00	—	24.00
Salad, 8½" . .	14.00	—	18.00
Sandwich, 14"	21.00	—	24.00
Sherbet,/Saucer	8.00	—	10.00
Relish Tray, 4 part	20.00	—	24.00

Relish Tray
with inserts . .	60.00	—	65.00
Relish Tray Insert	4.00	—	5.00
S & P Shakers, sq.	35.00	—	40.00
Sherbet	8.00	—	10.00
Tumbler, ftd. 10 oz.	20.00	—	22.00
Vase, 8"	20.00	—	25.00
Wine, 3½"	6.00	—	8.00

MANHATTON — PINK

Bowls —
Berry, h., 5 3/8"	17.00	—	20.00
Berry, 7½" . .	16.00	—	18.00
Closed handles	22.00	—	27.00
Fruit, 9½" . .	25.00	—	35.00
Candy Dish, 3 legs	12.00	—	15.00
Comport, 5¾" . .	30.00	—	35.00
Creamer	12.00	—	14.00
Sugar, open . .	12.00	—	14.00

Pitcher —
Tilt, 80 oz. . .	55.00	—	65.00

Relish Tray
with inserts . .	60.00	—	65.00
Relish Tray Insert	5.00	—	6.00
S & P Shakers, sq.	50.00	—	55.00
Sherbet	12.00	—	15.00
Tumbler, ftd. 10 oz.	20.00	—	22.00

MAYFAIR – BLUE

Bowls –

Cereal, 5½" . .	55.00	—	60.00
Flat, low, 11¾"	80.00	—	85.00
Fruit, sc. 12"	80.00	—	85.00
Vegetable, 10"	75.00	—	80.00
Veg. cvd. 10"	125.00	—	130.00
Butter Dish, cvd.	. . . .		325.00
Creamer, ftd. . .	75.00	—	80.00
Sugar, open . .	85.00	—	90.00

Pitchers –

60 oz. 8"	175.00	—	200.00
80 oz. 8½" . .	200.00	—	225.00

Plates –

5¾"	20.00	—	25.00
Dinner, 9½" . .	75.00	—	80.00
Grill, 9½" . .	40.00	—	45.00
Luncheon, 8½"	40.00	—	45.00
Off-centre			
indent, 6½" . .	25.00	—	30.00
Platter, o.h. oval	55.00	—	65.00
Relish, 4 part . .	55.00	—	65.00
Shaker, one	140.00	—	155.00
Sherbet, ftd. 4¾"	75.00	—	85.00
Vase, sweet pea . .	110.00	—	120.00

MAYFAIR – PINK

Bowls –

Cereal, 5½" . .	27.00	—	32.00
Cream Soup, 5"	50.00	—	55.00
Flat, low, 11¾"	70.00	—	75.00
Fruit, sc. 12"	65.00	—	70.00
Vegetable, 7"	25.00	—	30.00
Veg. cvd. 7" . .	65.00	—	75.00
Vegetable, 10"	30.00	—	35.00
Veg, cvd. 10"	95.00	—	110.00
Butter Dish, cvd.	65.00	—	75.00
Cake Plate, ftd. 10"	35.00	—	40.00
Candy, cvd.	65.00	—	75.00
Celery Dish, 10"	35.00	—	40.00
Cookie Jar, cvd. . .	55.00	—	60.00
Creamer, ftd. . .	25.00	—	28.00
Sugar, open . .	20.00	—	25.00

MAYFAIR – PINK

Cup	20.00	—	25.00
Saucer, with			
cup ring	35.00	—	40.00
Decanter & Stopper	135.00	—	150.00

Goblets –

Cocktail, 3 oz.	80.00	—	85.00
Water, 9 oz. . .	70.00	—	80.00
Wine, 3 oz. . .	100.00	—	110.00

Pitchers –

37 oz. 6"	50.00	—	55.00
60 oz. 8"	50.00	—	55.00
80 oz. 8½" . .	85.00	—	105.00

Plates –

5¾"	13.00	—	15.00
Cake, h. 12" . .	45.00	—	50.00
Dinner, 9½" . .	50.00	—	55.00
Grill, 9½" . .	40.00	—	45.00
Lundheon, 8½"	25.00	—	35.00
Off-centre			
indent, 6½" . .	25.00	—	30.00
Sherbet, 6½" . .	14.00	—	16.00
Platter, o.h. oval	25.00	—	30.00
Relish, 4 part . .	30.00	—	35.00
S & P Shakers, pr	65.00	—	75.00
Sandwich server . .	48.00	—	55.00
Sherbet, fl. 2¼" . .	170.00	—	180.00
Sherbet, ftd. 3" . .	20.00	—	23.00

Tumblers –

Iced Tea, 13½ oz.	50.00	—	60.00
Juice, 5 oz. . .	45.00	—	55.00
Water, 9 oz. . .	30.00	—	35.00
Footed, 10 oz.	40.00	—	50.00
Footed, Iced			
Tea, 15 oz. . .	45.00	—	50.00
Footed, Juice	85.00	—	95.00
Vase, sweet pea . .	140.00	—	165.00
Whiskey, 1½ oz. . .	75.00	—	85.00

MISS AMERICA — CRYSTAL

Bowls —

Cereal, 6¼"			11.00
Curved, 8" . .	45.00	—	50.00
Fruit,straight,8¾"	40.00	—	50.00
Vegetable, oval	15.00	—	20.00
Cake Plate, ftd. 12"	30.00	—	35.00
Celery Dish, 10½"	13.00	—	15.00
Coaster, 5¾" . .	17.00	—	20.00
Comport, 5"	16.00	—	18.00
Creamer, ftd. . .	10.00	—	12.00
Sugar, open . .	10.00	—	12.00
Cup	10.00	—	12.00
Saucer	4.00	—	5.00

Goblets —

Juice, 5 oz. . .	30.00	—	35.00
Water, 10 oz.	25.00	—	30.00
Wine, 3 oz. . .	25.00	—	30.00
Pitcher, 65 oz. 8"	65.00	—	70.00

Plates —

Dinner, 10¼"	15.00	—	18.00
Grill, 10¼" . .	12.00	—	15.00
Salad, 8½" . .	8.00	—	10.00
Sherbet, 5¾"	5.00	—	6.00
Platter, oval, 12¼"	16.00	—	20.00
Relish, 4 part . .	12.00	—	16.00
Relish, dvided			
Relish, div. 11¾"	20.00	—	30.00
S & P Shakers, pr.	35.00	—	40.00
Sherbet	9.00	—	11.00

Tumblers —

Iced Tea, 14 oz.	30.00	—	35.00
Juice, 5 oz. . .	20.00	—	25.00
Water, 10 oz.	20.00	—	25.00

MISS AMERICA — PINK

Bowls —

Cereal, 6¼"			35.00
Curved, 8" . .	75.00	—	85.00
Fruit,straight,8¾"	60.00	—	70.00
Vegetable, oval	30.00	—	35.00
Cake Plate, ftd. 12"	45.00	—	50.00
Candy, cvd.	125.00	—	135.00
Celery Dish, 10½"	25.00	—	30.00
Coaster, 5¾" . .	25.00	—	30.00
Creamer, ftd. . .	20.00	—	25.00
Sugar, open . .	20.00	—	25.00
Cup	25.00	—	30.00
Saucer, ...			6.00

Goblet —

Water, 10 oz.	50.00	—	55.00

Plates —

Dinner, 10¼"	25.00	—	30.00
Grill, 10¼" . .	25.00	—	30.00
Salad, 8½" . .	20.00	—	25.00
Sherbet, 5¾"	8.00	—	10.00
Platter, oval, 12¾"	25.00	—	30.00
Relish, 4 part . .	25.00	—	30.00
S & P Shakers, pr.	65.00	—	75.00
Sherbet	18.00	—	23.00

Tumblers —

Juice, 5 oz. . .	55.00	—	65.00
Water, 10 oz.	35.00	—	40.00

MODERNTONE — COBALT

Ash Tray with
    Match Holder 7¾" 130.00
Bowls —
    Berry, 5" . . . . 20.00 — 25.00
    Berry, 8¾" . . 50.00 — 55.00
    Cream Soup, 4¾" 20.00 — 25.00
Butter Dish,
    metal cover . . 100.00 — 115.00
Creamer . . . . . . 12.00 — 15.00
    Sugar, open . . 12.00 — 15.00
Cup . . . . 11.00 — 13.00
    Saucer . . . . 5.00 — 6.00
Custard . . . . . . 17.00 — 22.00
Plates —
    Dinner, 8 7/8" 15.00 — 20.00
    Luncheon, 7¾" 11.00 — 15.00
    Salad, 6¾" . . 11.00 — 15.00
    Sandwich, 10½" 45.00 — 55.00
    Sherbet, 5 7/8" 6.00
Punch Bowl/metal stand
    with 8 cups . . 200.00 — 225.00
S & P Shakers, pr. 45.00 — 50.00
Sherbet . . . . . . 15.00 — 20.00
Tumblers —
    5 oz. . . . . . . 40.00 — 45.00
    9 oz. . . . . . . 35.00 — 40.00
    12 oz. . . . . 100.00 — 110.00
Whiskey, 1½ oz. . . 25.00 — 30.00

MOONSTONE — OPALESCENT HOBNAIL

Bon-Bon,
    heart shape . . 15.00 — 18.00
Bowls —
    Berry, 5½" . . 17.00 — 23.00
    Cloverleaf . . 15.00 — 17.00
    Crimped, 9½" 20.00 — 25.00
    Crimped, h, 6½" 15.00 — 18.00
    Dessert,
    crimped, 5½" 10.00 — 12.00
    Flat, 7¾" . . 14.00 — 17.00
Candle holders, pr 20.00 — 23.00
Candy, cvd. 6" . . 30.00 — 35.00
Cigarette Jar, cvd. 25.00 — 30.00
Creamer . . . . . . 10.00 — 12.00
    Sugar, open . . 10.00 — 12.00
Cup . . . . 10.00 — 12.00
    Saucer/Sherbet 4.00 — 6.00
Goblet, 10 oz. . . 20.00 — 25.00
Plates —
    Luncheon, 8" 15.00 — 18.00
    Sandwich, 10" 25.00 — 30.00
    Sherbet/Saucer 4.00 — 6.00
Puff Box, cvd. 4¾" 25.00 — 30.00
Relish, divided, 7¾" 14.00 — 16.00
Sherbet, ftd. . . . . 10.00 — 15.00
Vase, 5½" . . . . 12.00 — 15.00

MOROCCAN AMETHYST

Ash Trays —
Round, 3¼" . .	5.00	—	7.00
Square, 8" . .	12.00	—	15.00
Triangular, 6 7/8"	8.00	—	10.00

Bowls —
Fruit, Octagonal, 4¾"	8.00	—	10.00
Oval, 7¾" . .	13.00	—	17.00
Rectangular, 7¾"	13.00	—	17.00
Round, 6" . .	10.00	—	12.00
Square, deep, 5¾"	10.00	—	12.00
Candy, short, cvd.	20.00	—	25.00
Candy, tall, cvd. . .	20.00	—	25.00
Cocktail mixer, lipped, 6¼" with stirrer.	30.00	—	35.00

MOROCCAN AMETHYST

Cocktail Shaker, metal lid	30.00	—	35.00
Cup	5.00	—	7.00
Saucer			3.00

Goblets —
Juice, 5½ oz.	8.00	—	10.00
Sherbet, 7½'oz.	8.00	—	10.00
Water, 9 oz. . .	12.00	—	15.00
Wine, 4½ oz. . .	8.00	—	10.00
Ice Bucket, 6" . .	30.00	—	35.00

Plates —
5¾"	5.00	—	6.00
Dinner, 9¾" . .	8.00	—	10.00
Sandwich, 12"	12.00	—	15.00
Salad, 7¼" . .	8.00	—	10.00
Snack, fan shape	8.00	—	10.00

Tumblers —
Iced Tea, 16 oz.	15.00	—	20.00
Juice, 4 oz. . .	8.00	—	10.00
Old Fashioned, 8 oz.	12.00	—	15.00
Water, 9 oz. . .	11.00	—	13.00
Water, 11 oz.	11.00	—	13.00
Water, crinkled bottom, 11 oz.	15.00	—	17.00
Vase, 8½"	25.00	—	30.00

PARROT — GREEN

Bowls —
Berry, 5"	25.00	—	30.00
Berry, 8"	75.00	—	80.00
Soup, 7"	45.00	—	50.00
Vegetable, oval	55.00	—	60.00
Creamer	35.00	—	40.00
Sugar, open . .	35.00	—	40.00
Cup	35.00	—	40.00
Saucer	12.00	—	15.00

Plates —
Dinner, 9" . .	50.00	—	55.00
Grill, rd. 10½"	35.00	—	40.00
Salad, 7½" . .	35.00	—	40.00
Sherbet, 5¾"	35.00	—	40.00
Platter, oblong, 11¼"	45.00	—	50.00
Sherbet, ftd.	25.00	—	30.00

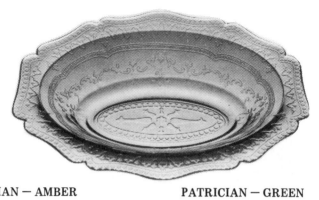

PATRICIAN – AMBER

Bowls –
Berry, 4¾"	. .	12.00	—	15.00
Berry, 8½"	. .	50.00	—	55.00
Cereal, 6"	. .	25.00	—	30.00
Cream Soup, 4¾"		18.00	—	20.00
Vegetable, oval		30.00	—	35.00
Butter Dish, cvd.		100.00	—	110.00
Cookie, cvd.		100.00	—	110.00
Creamer		11.00	—	13.00
Sugar, cvd.	. .	75.00	—	80.00
Sugar, open	. .	11.00	—	13.00
Cup		10.00	—	12.00
Saucer		10.00	—	12.00
Jam Dish		30.00	—	35.00

Pitcher, applied handle,
75 oz. 8¼"	. .	125.00	—	135.00

Plates –
Dinner, 10½"		9.00	—	12.00
Grill, 10½"	. .	15.00	—	20.00
Luncheon, 9"		12.00	—	15.00
Salad, 7½"	. .	15.00	—	20.00
Sherbet, 6"	. .	10.00	—	12.00
Platter, oval, 11½"		35.00	—	40.00
S & P Shakers, pr.		65.00	—	70.00
Sherbet		12.00	—	15.00

Tumblers –
5 oz. 4"		30.00	—	35.00
9 oz. 4¼"	. .	30.00	—	35.00
14 oz. 5½"	. .	45.00	—	50.00
Ftd. 8 oz. 5¼"		55.00	—	60.00

PATRICIAN – GREEN

Bowls –
Berry, 4¾"	. .	12.00	—	15.00
Berry, 8½"	. .	40.00	—	45.00
Cereal, 6"	. .	30.00	—	35.00
Cream Soup, 4¾"		20.00	—	25.00
Vegetable, oval		25.00	—	30.00
Butter Dish, cvd.		120.00	—	130.00
Creamer		13.00	—	15.00
Sugar, cvd.	. .	75.00	—	80.00
Sugar, open	. .	10.00	—	12.00
Cup		10.00	—	12.00
Saucer		10.00	—	12.00
Jam Dish		35.00	—	40.00

Pitcher, applied handle,
75 oz. 8¼"	. .	125.00	—	135.00

Plates –
Dinner, 10½"		40.00	—	45.00
Grill, 10½"	. .	15.00	—	20.00
Luncheon, 9"		12.00	—	15.00
Salad, 7½"	. .	15.00	—	20.00
Sherbet, 6"	. .	10.00	—	12.00
Platter, oval, 11½"		25.00	—	30.00
S & P Shakers, pr.		75.00	—	80.00
Sherbet		15.00	—	17.00

Tumblers –
5 oz. 4"		35.00	—	40.00
9 oz. 4¼"	. .	30.00	—	35.00
14 oz. 5½"	. .	45.00	—	50.00
Ftd. 8 oz. 5¼"		55.00	—	60.00

Not illustrated —
PETALWARE — CREMAX, MONAX, FLORETTE — fired-on decoration.

Bowls —

Berry, 9"	25.00	—	30.00
Cereal, 5¾" . .	12.00	—	14.00
Cream Soup, 4½"	12.00	—	14.00
Creamer	12.00	—	14.00
Sugar, open . .	12.00	—	14.00
Cup	10.00	—	12.00
Saucer	3.00	—	4.00

Plates —

Dinner, 9" . .	10.00	—	15.00
Salad, 8"	10.00	—	12.00
Salver, 11¾" . .	25.00	—	30.00
Sherbet, 6" . .	6.00	—	8.00
Platter, oval, 13"	25.00	—	30.00
Sherbet, ftd. 4½"	12.00	—	14.00

Not illustrated —
PETALWARE — MONAX PLAIN

Bowls —

Berry, 9"	17.00	—	20.00
Cereal, 5¾" . .	6.00	—	8.00
Cream Soup, 4½"	10.00	—	12.00
Soup, 7"	60.00	—	65.00
Creamer	6.00	—	8.00
Sugar, open . .	6.00	—	8.00
Cup	6.00	—	8.00
Saucer	2.00	—	3.00
Sugar, open . .	6.00	—	8.00
Cup	6.00	—	8.00
Saucer	2.00	—	3.00

Plates —

Dinner, 9" . . .	6.00	—	8.00
Salad, 8"	4.00	—	5.00
Salver, 11¾" . .	10.00	—	12.00
Sherbet, 6" . .	3.00	—	4.00
Platter, oval, 13"	17.00	—	20.00
Sherbet, ftd. 4" . .	30.00	—	35.00
Sherbet, ftd. 4½"	8.00	—	10.00

PRETZEL — CRYSTAL

Bowls —

Berry, 9 3/8"	15.00	—	20.00
Coupe Soup, 7½"	12.00	—	15.00
Fruit Cup, 4½"	5.00	—	6.00
Celery Tray, 10¼"	5.00	—	7.00
Creamer	6.00	—	8.00
Sugar, open . .	7.00	—	9.00
Cup	6.00	—	8.00
Saucer			4.00
Olive Dish, leaf shape, 7"	5.00	—	6.00
Pickle Dish, two handles, 8½"	6.00	—	8.00

Plates —

6"			3.00
Dinner, 9 3/8"	8.00	—	12.00
Salad, 8 3/8"	6.00	—	8.00
Sandwich, 11½"	12.00	—	15.00
Square, 7¼" . .	10.00	—	12.00
Tab handles, 6"			3.00

Tumblers —

5 oz. 3½" . .	25.00	—	30.00
9 oz. 4½" . .	25.00	—	30.00
12 oz., 5½" . .	35.00	—	40.00

PRINCESS — GREEN

Ash Tray, ...	85.00	—	90.00
Bowls —			
Berry, 4½" . .	30.00	—	35.00
Cereal, 5" . .	35.00	—	40.00
Hat Shape, 9½"	40.00	—	45.00
Salad, 9"	35.00	—	40.00
Vegetable, oval	25.00	—	30.00
Butter Dish, cvd.	110.00	—	115.00
Cake Stand, 10"	25.00	—	30.00
Candy, cvd.	60.00	—	65.00
Coaster	40.00	—	45.00
Cookie Jar, cvd. . .	60.00	—	65.00
Creamer	18.00	—	20.00
Sugar, cvd.	35.00	—	40.00
Sugar, open . .	15.00	—	20.00
Cup	10.00	—	15.00
Saucer	6.00	—	9.00
Pitchers —			
37 oz. 6 " . .	45.00	—	55.00
60 oz. 8"	55.00	—	60.00
Plates —			
Dinner, 9½" . .	25.00	—	30.00
Grill, 9½" . .	15.00	—	18.00
Grill, c.h. 10½"	12.00	—	15.00
Salad, 8"	15.00	—	18.00
Sandwich, 10¼"	15.00	—	20.00
Sherbet/Saucer	6.00	—	9.00
Platter, c.h. 12" . .	25.00	—	30.00
Relish, divided, . .	30.00	—	35.00
S & P Shakers, 4½"	60.00	—	65.00
Spice Shakers, 5½"	55.00	—	60.00
Sherbet, ftd.	25.00	—	30.00
Tumblers —			
Ftd. 10 oz. . .	35.00	—	40.00
Ftd. 12½ oz. . .	105.00	—	115.00
Iced Tea, 13 oz.	45.00	—	50.00
Juice, 5 oz. . .	30.00	—	35.00
Water, 9 oz. . .	30.00	—	35.00
Vase, 8"	40.00	—	45.00

PRINCESS — PINK

Bowls —			
Berry, 4½" . .	23.00	—	27.00
Cereal, 5" . .	25.00	—	30.00
Hat Shape, 9½"	25.00	—	30.00
Salad, 9"	25.00	—	30.00
Vegetable, oval	22.00	—	26.00
Butter Dish, cvd.	110.00	—	115.00
Cake Stand, 10"	25.00	—	30.00
Candy, cvd.	60.00	—	65.00
Cookie Jar, cvd. . .	65.00	—	70.00
Creamer	18.00	—	20.00
Sugar, covd. . .	30.00	—	35.00
Cup	10.00	—	15.00
Saucer/Sherbet	6.00	—	9.00
Pitchers —			
37 oz. 6"	45.00	—	55.00
60 oz. 8"	55.00	—	60.00
Plates —			
Dinner, 9½" . .	20.00	—	25.00
Grill, 9½" . .	15.00	—	18.00
Grill, c.h.10½"	12.00	—	14.00
Salad, 8"	15.00	—	18.00
Sandwich,10¼"	13.00	—	15.00
Sherbet/Saucer	6.00	—	9.00
Platter, c.h. 12" . .	25.00	—	30.00
Relish, divided . .	25.00	—	30.00
S & P Shakers, 4½"	55.00	—	60.00
Sherbet, ftd.	15.00	—	20.00
Tumblers —			
Ftd. 10 oz. . .	25.00	—	30.00
Iced Tea, 13 oz.	25.00	—	30.00
Juice, 5 oz. . .	25.00	— -	30.00
Water, 9 oz. . .	23.00	—	28.00
Vase, 8"	30.00	—	35.00

PRINCESS — TOPAZ

Bowls —			
Berry, 4½" . .	55.00	—	60.00
Cereal, 5" . .	35.00	—	40.00
Vegetable, oval	65.00	—	70.00
Creamer	18.00	—	20.00
Sugar, cvd. . .	40.00	—	45.00
Sugar, open . .	12.00	—	15.00
Cup	10.00	—	15.00
Saucer/Sherbet	5.00	—	7.00
Pitcher, 60 oz. 8"	100.00	—	110.00
Plates —			
Dinner, 9½" . .	18.00	—	23.00
Grill, 9½" . .	15.00	—	18.00
Grill, c.h. 10½"	8.00	—	10.00
Salad, 8"	11.00	—	13.00
Sherbet/Saucer	5.00	—	7.00
Platter, c.h. 12" . .	70.00	—	75.00
S & P Shakers, 4½"	80.00	—	85.00
Sherbet, ftd.	40.00	—	45.00
Tumblers —			
Ftd. 10 oz. . .	25.00	—	30.00
Iced Tea, 13 oz.	30.00	—	35.00
Juice, 5 oz. . .	30.00	—	35.00
Water, 9 oz. . .	25.00	—	30.00

QUEEN MARY — CRYSTAL

Ash Trays —
Oval, 2 x 3¾ . .	3.00	—	4.00
Round, 3½" . .	3.00	—	4.00

Bowls —
7"	8.00	—	10.00
Berry, 4"	4.00	—	5.00
Berry, 4½" . .	4.00	—	5.00
Berry, 5"	4.00	—	5.00
Berry, 8¾" . .	12.00	—	14.00
Cereal, 6" . .	7.00	—	9.00
Two handles, 5½"	6.00	—	8.00

Butter/Preserve
Dish, cvd. . .	25.00	—	30.00
Candy, cvd.	20.00	—	25.00

Candlesticks, double
branch, 4½" pr.	18.00	—	22.00
Celery/Pickle Dish	10.00	—	12.00
Cigarette Jar, oval	6.00	—	8.00
Coaster, 3½"			3.00
Coaster/Ash Tray, 4¼"	5.00	—	7.00
Comport, 5¾" . .	8.00	—	10.00
Creamer, oval . .	6.00	—	8.00
Sugar, open . .	5.00	—	6.00
Cup	6.00	—	8.00
Saucer.	3.00	—	4.00

Plates —
Dinner, 9¾" . .	15.00	—	20.00
Sandwich, 12"	10.00	—	12.00
Salad, 8¾" . .	6.00	—	8.00
Serving, 14" . .	12.00	—	15.00
Sherbet, 6" or 6 5/8"			5.00
Relish, 3 part, 12"	10.00	—	12.00
Relish, 4 part, 14"	12.00	—	15.00
S & P Shakers, pr.	25.00	—	30.00
Sherbet, ftd.	4.00	—	6.00

Tumblers —
Ftd. 10 oz. . .	45.00	—	50.00
Juice, 5 oz. . .	5.00	—	6.00
Water, 9 oz. . .	6.00	—	8.00

QUEEN MARY — PINK

Ash Tray —
Oval, 2 x 3¾"	6.00	—	8.00

Bowls —
7"	12.00	—	15.00
Berry, 4"	5.00	—	6.00
Berry, 4½" . .	6.00	—	8.00
Berry, 5"	6.00	—	8.00
Berry, 8¾" . .	18.00	—	20.00
Cereal, 6" . .	25.00	—	30.00
Two handles, 5½"	25.00	—	30.00

Butter/Preserve
Dish, cvd. . .	130.00	—	140.00
Candy, cvd.	40.00	—	45.00

Celery/Pickle
Dish, 5 x 10 . .	25.00	—	30.00
Cigarette Jar, oval	7.00	—	9.00
Coaster, 3½" . .	4.00	—	5.00
Comport, 5¾" . .	10.00	—	13.00
Creamer, ftd. . .	20.00	—	25.00
Sugar, open . .	25.00	—	30.00
Creamer, oval . .	8.00	—	10.00
Sugar, open . .	6.00	—	8.00
Cup	6.00	—	9.00
Saucer	3.00	—	4.00

Plates —
Dinner, 9¾" . .	45.00	—	50.00
Sandwich, 12"	15.00	—	20.00
Serving, 14" . .	18.00	—	22.00
Sherbet, 6" or 6 5/8"			6.00
Relish, 3 part, 12"	15.00	—	12.00
Relish, 4 part, 14"	15.00	—	20.00
Sherbet, ftd.	5.00	—	7.00

Tumblers —
Ftd. 10 oz. 5"	45.00	—	50.00
Juice, 5oz. . .	10.00	—	13.00
Water, 9 oz. . .	12.00	—	15.00

ROULETTE — CRYSTAL

Bowl —
Fruit, 9"	12.00	—	14.00

Cup . . . . 40.00 — 50.00
    Saucer . . . . 3.00 — 4.00

Pitcher —
    65 oz., 8" . . 30.00 — 35.00

Plates —
    Luncheon, 8½" 6.00 — 7.00
    Sandwich, 12" 14.00 — 17.00
    Sherbet, 6" . . 4.00 — 5.00

Sherbet . . . . . . 4.00 — 5.00

Tumblers —
    Ftd. 10 oz. . . 17.00 — 20.00
    Iced Tea, 12 oz. 18.00 — 20.00
    Juice, 5 oz. . . 8.00 — 10.00
    Old Fashioned 30.00 — 35.00
    Water, 9 oz. . . 15.00 — 17.00

Whiskey, 1½ oz. . . 8.00 — 10.00

ROULETTE — GREEN/PINK

Bowl —
    Fruit, 9" . . . . 15.00 — 17.00

Cup . . . . 6.00 — 8.00
    Sauce_ . . . . 3.00 — 4.00

Pitcher —
    65 oz. 8" . . . . 40.00 — 45.00

Plates —
    Luncheon, 8½" 7.00 — 8.00
    Sandwich, 12" 14.00 — 17.00
    Sherbet, 6" . . 5.00 — 6.00

Sherbet . . . . . . 7.00 — 8.00

Tumblers —
    Ftd. 10 oz. . . 25.00 — 30.00
    Iced Tea, 12 oz. 25.00 — 30.00
    Juice, 5 oz. . . 23.00 — 27.00
    Old Fashioned 45.00 — 50.00
    Water, 9 oz. . . 25.00 — 30.00

Whiskey, 1½ oz. . . 15.00 — 17.00

ROYAL LACE — CRYSTAL
Bowls —

Berry, 5"	15.00	—	18.00
Berry, 10" . .	20.00	—	23.00
Cream Soup. 4¾"	12.00	—	14.00
Ruffled edge,			
3 legs, 10" . .	30.00	—	35.00
Straight edge,			
3 legs, 10" . .	20.00	—	23.00
Vegetable, oval	25.00	—	30.00
Butter Dish, cvd.	80.00	—	90.00
Candlesticks —			
Rolled edge, pr	50.00	—	60.00
Ruffled edge, pr	35.00	—	40.00
Straight edge, pr.	35.00	—	40.00
Cookie Jar, cvd. . .	40.00	—	45.00
Creamer, ftd. . .	15.00	—	17.00
Sugar, cvd. . .	30.00	—	35.00
Sugar, open . .	10.00	—	12.00
Cup	8.00	—	10.00
Saucer	4.00	—	5.00
Pitchers —			
64 oz. 8"	50.00	—	55.00
86 oz. 8"	60.00	—	65.00
Ice Lip, 68 oz.	60.00	—	65.00
Straight sides,			
48 oz.	45.00	—	50.00
Plates —			
Dinner, 9 7/8"	15.00	—	17.00
Grill, 9"	12.00	—	14.00
Luncheon, 8½"	9.00	—	11.00
Sherbet, 6" . .	4.00	—	5.00
Platter, oval, 13"	20.00	—	23.00
S & P Shakers, pr	50.00	—	55.00
Sherbet, ftd.	10.00	—	12.00
Sherbet in metal			
holder	4.00	—	5.00
Tumblers —			
5 oz. 3½" . .	20.00	—	22.00
9 oz. 4 1/8" . .	13.00	—	15.00
10 oz. 4 7/8"	20.00	—	25.00
12 oz. 5 3/8"	20.00	—	25.00

ROYAL LACE — COBALT
Bowls —

Berry, 5"	50.00	—	60.00
Berry, 10" . .	65.00	—	70.00
Cream Soup, 4¾"	40.00	—	45.00
Straight edge,			
3 legs, 10" . .	65.00	—	75.00
Vegetable, oval	60.00	—	65.00
Butter Dish, cvd.	. . . .		600.00
Cookie Jar, cvd.	. . . .		425.00
Creamer, ftd. . .	50.00	—	60.00
Sugar, ftd. open	35.00	—	40.00
Sugar lid	180.00	—	200.00
Cup	35.00	—	40.00
Saucer	13.00	—	15.00
Pitcher —			
Straight sides, 48 oz.	. . . .		115.00
Plates —			
Dinner, 9 7/8"	40.00	—	45.00
Grill, 9"	40.00	—	45.00
Luncheon, 8½"	40.00	—	45.00
Sherbet, 6" . .	15.00	—	18.00
Platter, oval, 13"	65.00	—	70.00
S & P Shakers, pr	275.00	—	300.00
Sherbet, ftd.	55.00	—	60.00
Tumblers —			
5 oz. 3½" . .	50.00	—	60.00
9 oz. 4 1/8" . .	50.00	—	55.00
10 oz. 4 7/8"	80.00	—	85.00

ROYAL LACE – GREEN

Bowls –

Berry, 5"	35.00	—	40.00
Berry, 10" . .	35.00	—	40.00
Cream Soup, 4¾"	35.00	—	40.00
Ruffled edge, 3 legs, 10" . .	70.00	—	75.00
Straight edge, 3 legs, 10" . .	45.00	—	50.00
Vegetable, oval	35.00	—	40.00
Butter Dish, cvd.	. . . .		325.00

Candlesticks –

Rolled edge,pr.	75.00	—	80.00
Ruffled edge,pr.	70.00	—	75.00
Straight edge,pr.	70.00	—	75.00
Cookie Jar, cvd. . .	90.00	—	95.00
Creamer, ftd. . . .	25.00	—	30.00
Sugar, cvd. . .	70.00	—	75.00
Sugar, open . .	25.00	—	30.00
Cup	25.00	—	28.00
Saucer	5.00	—	7.00

Plates –

Dinner, 9 7/8"	25.00	—	30.00
Grill, 9"	25.00	—	30.00
Luncheon, 8½"	15.00	—	18.00
Sherbet, 6" . .	10.00	—	12.00
Platter, oval, 13"	40.00	—	45.00
S & P Shakers, pr	150.00	—	165.00
Sherbet, ftd.	25.00	—	30.00

Tumblers –

5 oz. 3½" . .	30.00	—	35.00
9 oz. 4 1/8" . .	30.00	—	35.00

ROYAL LACE – PINK

Bowls –

Berry, 5"	30.00	—	35.00
Berry, 10" . .	30.00	—	35.00
Cream Soup, 4¾"	20.00	—	25.00
Rolled edge, 3 legs, 10" . .	45.00	—	50.00
Ruffled edge, 3 legs, 10" . .	45.00	—	50.00
Straight edge, 3 legs, 10" . .	35.00	—	40.00
Vegetable, oval	30.00	—	35.00
Butter Dish, cvd.	165.00	—	180.00

Candlesticks –

Rolled edge, pr.	60.00	—	65.00
Ruffled edge, pr	60.00	—	65.00
Straight edge,pr.	45.00	—	50.00
Cookie Jar, cvd. . .	60.00	—	65.00
Creamer, ftd. . .	18.00	—	23.00
Sugar, cvd. . .	45.00	—	50.00
Sugar, open . .	15.00	—	20.00
Cup	15.00	—	17.00
Saucer	7.00	—	8.00

Pitchers –

64 oz. 8"	100.00	—	110.00
86 oz. 8"	110.00	—	120.00
Ice Lip, 96 oz.	115.00	—	125.00
Straight sides, 48 oz.	65.00	—	70.00

Plates –

Dinner, 9 7/8"	20.00	—	25.00
Grill, 9"	17.00	—	20.00
Luncheon, 8½"	17.00	—	20.00
Sherbet, 6" . .	7.00	—	9.00
Platter, oval, 13"	30.00	—	35.00
S & P Shakers, pr.	65.00	—	75.00
Sherbet, ftd.	20.00	—	25.00

Tumblers –

5 oz. 3½" . .	22.00	—	25.00
9 oz. 4 1/8" . .	18.00	—	22.00

SHARON — AMBER

Bowls —

Berry, 5"	9.00	—	11.00
Berry, 8½" . .	9.00	—	12.00
Cereal, 6" . .	18.00	—	32.00
Cream Soup, 5"	30.00	—	33 00
Flat Soup, 7½"	50.00	—	55.00
Fruit, 10½" . .	25.00	—	30.00
Vegetable, oval	18.00	—	22.00
Butter Dish, cvd.	60.00	—	70.00
Cake Plate ftd. 11½"	25.00	—	30.00
Candy, cvd.	55.00	—	65.00
Creamer ftd. . .	16.00	—	18.00
Sugar, cvd. . .	40.00	—	45.00
Sugar, open . .	13.00	—	15.00
Cup	11.00	—	13.00
Saucer	6.00	—	7.00
Jam Dish, 7½" . .	40.00	—	45.00
Pitcher, 80 oz. . .	150.00	—	160.00

Plates —

Bread & Butter	5.00	—	7.00
Dinner, 9½" . .	13.00	—	15.00
Salad, 7½" . .	15.00	—	18.00
Plater, oval, 12" . .	18.00	—	20.00
S & P Shakers, pr.	55.00	—	60.00
Sherbet, ftd.	14.00	—	16.00

SHARON — GREEN

Bowls —

Berry, 5"	14.00	—	16.00
Berry 8½" . .	35.00	—	40.00
Cereal, 6" . .	25.00	—	30.00
Cream Soup, 5"	50.00	—	60.00
Fruit, 10½" . .	40.00	—	45.00
Vegetable, oval	30.00	—	35.00
Butter Dish, cvd.	100.00	—	110.00
Cake Plate, ftd. 11½"	65.00	—	70.00
Creamer, ftd. . .	25.00	—	30.00
Sugar, cvd. . .	60.00	—	65.00
Sugar, open . .	14.00	—	16.00
Cup	20.00	—	23.00
Saucer	6.00	—	9.00
Jam Dish, 7½" . .	50.00	—	55.00

SHARON — GREEN

Plates —

Bread & Butter	8.00	—	9.00
Dinner, 9½" . .	20.00	—	23.00
Salad, 7½" . .	25.00	—	30.00
Platter, oval, 12"	25.00	—	30.00
S & P Shakers, pr.	25.00	—	30.00
Sherbet, ftd.	40.00	—	45.00

Tumbler —

Thick/Thin, 9 oz.		70.00

SHARON — PINK

Bowls —

Berry, 5"	12.00	—	15.00
Berry, 8½" . .	25.00	—	30.00
Cereal, 6" . .	22.00	—	26.00
Cream Soup, 5"	50.00	—	55.00
Flat Soup, 7½"	50.00	—	55.00
Fruit, 10½" . .	40.00	—	50.00
Vegetable, oval	25.00	—	30.00
Butter Dish, cvd.	60.00	—	65.00
Cake Plate, ftd. 11½"	40.00	—	45.00
Candy, cvd.	55.00	—	60.00
Creamer, ftd. . .	20.00	—	23.00
Sugar, ftd. cvd.	40.00	—	45.00
Sugar, ftd. open	13.00	—	15.00
Creamer ftd. . .	20.00	—	23.00
Sugar, cvd. . .	40.00	—	45.00
Sugar, open . .	13.00	—	15.00
Cup	17.00	—	20.00
Saucer	9.00	—	11.00
Pitcher, 80 oz. . .	155.00	—	165.00

Plates —

Bread & Butter	5.00	—	7.00
Dinner, 9½" . .	20.00	—	25.00
Salad, 7½" . .	25.00	—	30.00
Platter, oval, 12"	20.00	—	25.00
S & P Shakers, pr.	55.00	—	65.00
Sherbet, ftd.	15.00	—	18.00

Tumbler —

Thick/Thin, 9 oz.	35.00	—	45.00

SWIRL — DELPHITE

Bowls —
Cereal, 5¼"	. .	14.00	— 16.00
Salad, 9"	. . . .	35.00	— 40.00

Candle Holders —
Single branch, pr	125.00	— 140.00
Creamer, ftd.	. .	12.00	— 15.00
Sugar, open	. .	10.00	— 12.00
Cup	. . . .	10.00	— 12.00
Saucer	. . . .	4.00	— 5.00

Plates —
10½"	. . . . . .	20.00	— 23.00
Dinner, 9¼"	. .	12.00	— 15.00
Salad, 8"	. . . .	9.00	— 11.00
Sherbet, 6½"		5.00	— 6.00
Platter, oval, 12"		40.00	— 45.00
Tray, handled, 10½"	30.00	— 35.00

SWIRL — PINK

Bowls —
Cereal, 5¼"	. .	11.00	— 13.00
Console, 10½"		25.00	— 30.00
Footed, c.h.	. .	25.00	— 30.00
Salad, 9"	. . . .	15.00	— 18.00
Salad, rimmed		20.00	— 23.00
Soup, tab handles	25.00	— 30.00
Butter Dish, cvd.	. . . .	— 225.00
Candy, open	. . . .	12.00	— 15.00
Candy, cvd.	. . . .	100.00	— 110.00
Coaster	. . . . .	8.00	— 11.00
Creamer, ftd.	. .	6.00	— 8.00
Sugar, open	. .	11.00	— 13.00
Cup	. . . .	8.00	— 10.00
Saucer	. . . .	3.00	— 4.00

Plates —
7¼"	. . . . . .	8.00	— 10.00
Dinner, 9¼"	. .	12.00	— 15.00
Salad, 8"	. . .	9.00	— 11.00
Sandwich, 12½"	15.00	— 17.00
Sherbet, 6½"		5.00	— 6.00
Sherbet, ftd.	. . . .	11.00	— 13.00

Tumblers —
9 oz. 4"	. . . .	15.00	— 18.00
9 oz. 4 5/8"	. .	20.00	— 23.00
13 oz. 5 1/8"		45.00	— 50.00
Ftd. 9 oz.	. .	18.00	— 22.00

Vase —
Ruffled, ftd. 6½"	18.00	— 22.00

SWIRL — ULTRAMARINE

Bowls —
Cereal, 5¼"	. .	15.00	— 18.00
Console, 10½"		30.00	— 35.00
Footed, c.h. 10"	35.00	— 40.00
Salad 9"	. . . .	25.00	— 30.00
Salad, rimmed		25.00	— 30.00
Soup, tab handles	30.00	— 35.00
Butter Dish, cvd.	275.00	— 300.00

Candle Holders —
Double branch, pr	. . . . . .	50.00
Candy, open	. . . .	20.00	— 25.00
Candy, cvd.	. . . .	135.00
Coaster	. . . . . .	12.00	— 15.00
Creamer, ftd.	. .	18.00	— 20.00
Sugar, open	. .	18.00	— 20.00
Cup	. . . .	18.00	— 20.00
Saucer	. . . .	4.00	— 5.00

Plates —
7¼"	. . . . . .	12.00	— 15.00
10½"	. . . . . .	35.00	— 40.00
Dinner, 9¼"	. .	18.00	— 20.00
Salad, 8"	. . . .	15.00	— 18.00
Sandwich, 12½"	25.00	— 30.00
Sherbet, 6½"		7.00	— 8.00
S & P Shakers, pr.	50.00	— 60.00
Sherbet, ftd.	. . . .	18.00	— 22.00

Tumblers —
9 oz., 4"	. . . .	35.00	— 40.00
Footed, 9 oz.		35.00	— 45.00

Vase —
Footed, 8½"	. .	30.00	— 35.00

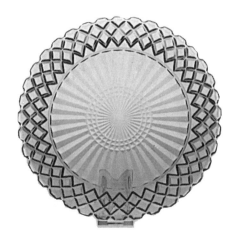

WATERFORD – CRYSTAL

Ash Tray, 4" ..	8.00	— 10.00
Bowls —		
Berry, 4¾" ..	7.00	— 9.00
Berry, 8¼" ..	11.00	— 14.00
Cereal, 5½" ..	18.00	— 22.00
Butter Dish, cvd.	30.00	— 35.00
Coaster, 4"	30.00	— 35.00
Creamer, oval ..	5.00	— 7.00
Sugar, oval, cvd.	10.00	— 12.00
Sugar, oval, open	5.00	— 7.00
Creamer, Miss Amer-		
ica style	40.00	— 45.00
Sugar, Miss Amer-		
ica style, open	40.00	— 45.00
Cup	6.00	— 8.00
Saucer	3.00	— 4.00
Goblets —		
5¼"	15.00	— 18.00
5 5/8"	15.00	— 18.00
Miss America		
style, 5½" ..	40.00	— 45.00
Lamp	35.00	— 40.00
Pitchers —		
Juice, tilt, 42 oz.	25.00	— 30.00
Ice lip, tilt, 80 oz.	40.00	— 45.00
Plates —		
Cake, handled	8.00	— 10.00
Dinner, 9 5/8"	8.00	— 10.00
Salad, 7 1 /8"	5.00	— 6.00
Sandwich, 13¾"	11.00	— 13.00
Sherbet, 6" ..	3.00	— 4.00
Relish, 5 part, 13¾"	20.00	— 23.00
S & P Shakers —		
2 styles, pr. ..	12.00	— 15.00
Sherbet, ftd.	5.00	— 6.00
Sherbet, ftd. sc. base	5.00	— 6.00
Tumbler —		
Ftd. 10 oz. 4 7/8"	12.00	— 15.00

WATERFORD – PINK

Bowls —		
Berry, 4¾" ..	10.00	— 15.00
Berry, 8¼" ..	18.00	— 22.00
Cereal, 5½" ..	30.00	— 35.00
Butter Dish, cvd.	225.00	— 250.00
Creamer, oval ..	10.00	— 13.00
Sugar, oval, cvd	35.00	— 40.00
Sugar, oval, open	11.00	— 13.00
Cup	15.00	— 18.00
Cup, Miss America		
style	40.00	— 45.00
Saucer	5.00	— 6.00
Plates —		
Cake, handled	18.00	— 20.00
Dinner, 9 5/8"	25.00	— 30.00
Salad, 7 1/8"	7.00	— 9.00
Sandwich, 13¾"	30.00	— 35.00
Sherbet, 6" ..	5.00	— 6.00
Sherbet, ftd.	15.00	— 18.00
Tumblers —		
Ftd. 10oz. 4 7/8"	20.00	— 25.00
Juice, Miss Amer-		
ica style, 5 oz.	70.00	— 75.00

WINDSOR — CRYSTAL

Ash Tray, 5¾" ..	15.00	—	18.00
Bowls —			
Berry, 4¾" ..	4.00	—	5.00
Berry, 8½" ..	8.00	—	10.00
Boat Shape ..	20.00	—	23.00
Cereal, 5 1/8"	10.00	—	12.00
Cream Soup, 5"	7.00	—	8.00
Fruit Console	30.00	—	35.00
Handles, 8" ..	8.00	—	10.00
Pointed Edge, 5"	5.00	—	6.00
Pointed Edge,8"	10.00	—	12.00
Pointed Edge,10½	30.00	—	35.00
Salad, 10½" ..	10.00	—	12.00
Three Legs, 7 1/8	9.00	—	11.00
Vegetable, oval	8.00	—	10.00
Butter Dish, cvd.	35.00	—	40.00
Cake Plate, ftd. ..	10.00	—	12.00
Candlesticks, 3" pr.	20.00	—	25.00
Candy, cvd.	20.00	—	25.00
Coaster, 3¼" ..	4.00	—	5.00
Comport	10.00	—	12.00
Creamer	5.00	—	7.00
Sugar, cvd. ..	8.00	—	10.00
Cup	4.00	—	5.00
Saucer	5.00	—	6.00
Pitchers —			
16 oz. 4½" ..	25.00	—	30.00
52 oz. 6¾" ..	15.00	—	18.00
Plates —			
Chop, 13 5/8"	10.00	—	12.00
Dinner, 9" ..	5.00	—	6.00
Salad, 7"	5.00	—	6.00
Sandwich, 10¼"	6.00	—	8.00
Sherbet, 6" ..	3.00	—	4.00
Platter, oval	7.00	—	9.00
Relish, divided ..	12.00	—	15.00
S & P Shakers, pr	20.00	—	25.00
Sherbet, ftd	4.00	—	5.00
Trays —			
4 x 4			7.00
4 x 4 handled			6.00
4 1/8 x 9			12.00
4 1 /8 x 9 handled			6.00
8½ x 9¾			18.00
8½ x 9¾ handled			10.00
Tumblers —			
Ftd. 4"	8.00	—	10.00
Ftd. 11 oz. 5"	10.00	—	12.00
Ftd. 7¼"	14.00	—	16.00
9 oz. 4"	7.00	—	8.00
12 oz. 5"	10.00	—	12.00

WINDSOR — GREEN

Ash Tray, 5¾" ..	55.00	—	65.00
Bowls —			
Berry, 4¾" ..	11.00	—	14.00
Beryy, 8½" ..	18.00	—	20.00
Boat Shape ..	40.00	—	45.00
Cereal, 5 1/8"	20.00	—	25.00
Cream Soup, 5"	30.00	—	35.00
Handled, 8" ..	25.00	—	30.00
Vegetable, oval	25.00	—	30.00
Butter Dish, cvd.	100.00	—	110.00
Cake Plate, ftd. ..	20.00	—	25.00
Coaster, 3¼" ..	20.00	—	25.00
Creamer	12.00	—	15.00
Sugar, cvd. ..	35.00	—	40.00
Sugar, open ..	10.00	—	12.00
Cup	11.00	—	13.00
Saucer	5.00	—	6.00
Pitcher, 52 oz. 6¾"	60.00	—	65.00
Plates —			
Chop, 13 5/8"	45.00	—	55.00
Dinner, 9" ..	20.00	—	25.00
Salad, 7"	22.00	—	25.00
Sandwich, 10¼"	18.00	—	20.00
Sherbet, 6" ..	7.00	—	9.00
Platter, oval, 11½"	20.00	—	25.00
S & P Shakers, pr.	60.00	—	65.00
Sherbet, ftd.	14.00	—	16.00
Trays —			
4 x 4 handled			14.00
4 1/8 x 9 handled			25.00
8½ x 9¾			50.00
8½ x 9¾ handled			40.00
Tumblers —			
9 oz. 4"	35.00	—	40.00
12 oz. 5"	50.00	—	55.00

188

WINDSOR — PINK

Ash Tray, 5¾" ..	40.00	— 50.00
Bowls —		
Berry, 4¾" ..	8.00	— 10.00
Berry, 8½" ..	18.00	— 20.00
Boat Shape ..	35.00	— 40.00
Cereal, 5 1/8"	20.00	— 25.00
Cream Soup, 5"	22.00	— 25.00
Fruit Console	95.00	— 110.00
Handled, 8" ..	25.00	— 30.00
Pointed Edge,5"	20.00	— 22.00
Pointed Edge,8"	45.00	— 50.00
Vegetable, oval	20.00	— 24.00
Butter Dish, cvd.	60.00	— 65.00
Cake Plate, ftd. 10¾"	20.00	— 25.00
Candlesticks, 3"pr.	85.00	— 95.00
Coaster, 3¼" ..	15.00	— 18.00
Creamer	14 00	— 17.00
Sugar, cvd. ..	25.00	— 30.00
Sugar, open ..	12.00	— 14.00
Cup	10.00	— 12.00
Saucer	5.00	— 6.00
Pitcher, 52 oz. 6¾"	30.00	— 35.00
Plates —		
Chop, 13 5/8"	40.00	— 50.00
Dinner, 9" ..	15.00	— 18.00
Salad, 7"	18.00	— 22.00
Sandwich, 10¼"	18.00	— 22.00
Sherbet, 6" ..	5.00	— 6.00
Platter, oval, 11½"	20.00	— 25.00
Powder Jar	65.00	— 70.00
S & P Shakers, pr.	40.00	— 50.00
Sherbet, ftd.	13.00	— 16.00
Trays —		
4 x 4		45.00
4 x 4 handled		12.00
4 1/8 x 9		60.00
4 1/8 x 9 handled		12.00
8½ x 9¾		95.00
8½ x 9¾ handled		28.00
Tumblers —		
9 oz. 4"	18.00	— 24.00
12 oz. 5"	30.00	— 35.00

MODERNTONE
LITTLE HOSTESS PARTY SET
16 Piece.

Cup, green, gray, chartreuse		
or burgundy ..	7.00	— 9.00
Saucer, green, gray or		
chartreuse ..	4.00	— 5.00
Plate, burgundy ..	6.00	— 7.00
Creamer, chartreuse	10.00	— 12.00
Sugar, chartreuse	10.00	— 12.00
Teapot, burgundy	30.00	— 35.00
Teapot lid,		
burgundy ..	35.00	— 40.00
Set	145.00	— 185.00
Set, boxed	155.00	— 210.00

The Little Hostess Party Sets came in five sets of different colour combinations. Pieces in each set come in specific colours. Colour combinations must be correct to form a set.

1) 16 Piece Set
Pink/Black/White

2) 16 Piece Set
Lemon/Beige/Pink/Aqua

3) 16 Piece Set
Gray/Rust/Gold/Turquoise

4) 16 Piece Set
Green/Gray/Chartreuse/
Burgundy   (illus.)

5 14 Piece Set
   No teapot and lid.
Pastels: Pink/Green/Blue/
Yellow

PRESSED GLASS

Pressed glass prices are for clear pieces in good condition with good impression and no chips, unless otherwise mentioned.

Coloured and opaque pieces usually bring higher prices.

ACADIAN

Butter Dish, cvd. . . $	140	-	150
Cake Plate	60	-	65
Celery Dish, h.	40	-	45
Comport, cvd.	140	-	150
Creamer	70	-	75
Nappy, no handles			20

Nappy, ribbed foot . .	20	-	25
Plate, diam. 7¼"	30	-	35
Plate, diam. 9"	40	-	45
Spooner	55	-	60
Sugar, cvd.	115	-	125

ACTRESS

Bowl, ftd. diam. 6" $	45	-	50
Bread Platter "Pinafore"	90	-	100
Butter Dish, cvd.	125	-	140
Cake Stand	130	-	140
Celery	85	-	95
Cheese Bell	250	-	275
Comport, cvd., high . .	175	-	200
Creamer	85	-	95
Goblet	140	-	150
Nappy, flat			20
Nappy, ftd.	20	-	25
Pickle Dish "Love's Request is Pickles"	65	-	70
Pickle Dish "Miss Neilson" . .	75	-	80
Pitcher, water	160	-	175
Spooner	65	-	70
Sugar, covered	115	-	125

ARCHED GRAPE

Butter Dish, cvd. . . $	70	-	75
Celery Vase	45	-	55
Comport, cvd.	110	-	120
Creamer	35	-	45
Goblet	50	-	55
Nappy			20
Pitcher, water	75	-	80
Spooner	25	-	30
Sugar, cvd.	75	-	80
Wine			35

AEGIS

Bowl, oval, 8" . . . . $	50	-	55
Butter Dish, cvd.	75	-	85
Comport, cvd.	105	-	115
Comport, open	60	-	65
Creamer	40	-	45
Goblet	110	-	120
Nappy, flat			20
Nappy, footed	20	-	25
Pitcher, water	70	-	75
Salt, footed			25
Spooner	35	-	40
Sugar, cvd.	65	-	75

ANDERSON

Butter Dish, cvd. . . $	75	-	85
Comport, cvd.	110	-	120
Creamer	55	-	65
Nappy, flat			20
Nappy, footed	20	-	25
Pitcher, water	100	-	110
Plate	35	-	40
Spooner	40	-	45
Sugar, cvd.	75	-	85

ATHENIAN

Butter Dish, cvd. . . $	70	-	75
Cake Stand	70	-	80
Comport, cvd.	85	-	95
Comport, open	45	-	50
Creamer, cvd.	85	-	95
Creamer, no lid	45	-	50
Jam/Marmalade	80	-	90
Pitcher, water	70	-	75
Salt & Pepper	65	-	75
Salt & Pepper, opaque	100	-	115
Sugar, cvd.	60	-	65
Tumbler	85	-	95

BARBERRY

Butter Dish, cvd. . . $	75 -	85
Cake Stand	55 -	60
Celery Vase	65 -	75
Comport, cvd. Ht. 10"	100 -	110
Creamer	35 -	45
Egg Cup	35 -	45
Goblet	50 -	55
Nappy		20
Pickle Dish	20 -	25
Pitcher, water	70 -	80
Spooner	30 -	35
Sugar, cvd.	65 -	70
Wine	45 -	50

BEADED ARCH

Butter Dish, cvd. . . $	65 -	70
Creamer	40 -	45
Goblet	70 -	80
Mugs	30 -	45
Pitcher, water	65 -	75
Relish Dish		20
Spooner	30 -	35
Sugar, cvd.	60 -	65

NOTE: Prices are for clear pieces, unless mentioned otherwise.
Coloured and opaque pieces usually bring higher prices.

BEADED BAND

Butter Dish, cvd. . . $	85 -	95
Cake Stand	50 -	55
Comport, cvd.	100 -	110
Creamer	45 -	50
Goblet	60 -	65
Nappy		20
Pitcher, water	75 -	85
Spooner	30 -	35
Sugar, cvd.	60 -	70
Syrup	130 -	140
Wine	50 -	60

BEADED GRAPE

Bowl, open, 7½" sq	$ 40	-	50
Butter Dish, cvd.	85	-	95
Cake Stand	85	-	95
Celery Tray	30	-	35
Comport, cvd.	100	-	115
Creamer	60	-	65
Goblet	100	-	110
Nappy			20
Pickle Dish	25	-	30
Plate, square	30	-	35
Pitcher, round	75	-	85
Pitcher, square	85	-	95
Platter/Bread Tray . .	60	-	65
Spooner	40	-	45
Sugar, cvd.	70	-	80
Tumbler	35	-	40
		Green + 25%	

BEADED OVAL & FAN NO. 2

Basket	$ 80	-	85
Bowls	25	-	45
Butter Dish, cvd.	80	-	85
Creamer	40	-	45
Goblet	250	-	275
Mug	30	-	35
Nappy, flat			20
Nappy, footed	20	-	25
Pitcher, water	80	-	85
Spooner	40	-	45
Sugar, cvd.	70	-	75

BEADED OVAL & FAN NO. 1

Butter Dish, cvd. . .	$ 70	-	80
Bowl, diam. 8¼"	25	-	30
Cake Stand	65	-	70
Creamer	35	-	40
Nappy			15
Pitcher water	75	-	85
Spooner	30	-	35
Sugar, cvd.	55	-	65

BEADED OVAL & SCROLL

Butter Dish, cvd. . .	$ 75	-	80
Comport, cvd.	80	-	90
Creamer	35	-	40
Goblet	70	-	75
Spooner	35	-	40
Sugar, cvd.	70	-	75

BEADED OVAL WINDOW

Butter Dish, cvd. $	85	- 95
Comport, cvd.	100	- 110
Comport, open, low . .	55	- 65
Creamer	50	- 55
Goblet, etched	115	- 125
Goblet, plain	75	- 85
Platter, bread	65	- 75
Spooner	40	- 45
Sugar, cvd.	70	- 75

BLACK EYED SUSAN

Butter Dish, cvd. . . $	100	- 110
Celery Vase	65	- 70
Cheese Bell		125
Comport, cvd.	120	- 130
Comport, open	70	- 75
Creamer	70	- 75
Spooner	45	- 50
Sugar, cvd.	80	- 90
Tumbler	45	- 50

BLEEDING HEART

Bowls . . . . $	30	- 45
Butter Dish, cvd.	80	- 85
Cake Stand	50	- 55
Comport, cvd., high . .	120	- 130
Creamer	45	- 50
Egg Cup	35	- 40
Goblet	70	- 80
Pickle Dish	35	- 40
Pitcher, water	105	- 115
Platter, bread	50	- 55
Spooner	45	- 50
Sugar, cvd.	65	- 70
Tumbler, flat	35	- 40
Wine	80	- 85

BLOCK

Butter Dish, cvd. . . $	70	- 80
Cake Stand	45	- 50
Celery Vase	35	- 40
Creamer	40	- 45
Goblet	50	- 55
Pitcher, water	80	- 90
Relish Dish		20
Spooner	35	- 40
Salt, master		20
Sugar, cvd.	55	- 60
Syrup	100	- 110
Tumbler	35	- 40
Vinegar/Oil Cruet . .	60	- 65
Wine	35	- 40

BUCKLE - LATE

Bowl, oval . . . . . . $	30	-	35
Butter Dish, cvd.	75	-	85
Cake Stand	55	-	60
Comport, cvd., small	85	-	95
Creamer	50	-	55
Goblet	70	-	75
Nappy, flat			20
Nappy, footed	25	-	30
Pitcher, water	85	-	95
Spooner	35	-	40
Sugar, cvd.	60	-	70
Wine	70	-	80

BOWTIE

Bowl, diam. 8" . . $	40	-	45
Butter Dish, cvd.	70	-	80
Cake Stand	70	-	80
Comport, open	55	-	60
Creamer	40	-	45
Nappy			15
Pitcher, water	65	-	70
Spooner	40	-	45
Sugar, cvd.	70	-	75

BUCKLE - EARLY

Creamer . . . . $	45	-	50
Egg Cup	50	-	55
Goblet	55	-	60
Nappy, flat			20
Nappy, footed	20	-	25
Spooner	40	-	45
Sugar, cvd.	70	-	80
Wine	50	-	55

BUCKLE & STAR

Butter Dish, cvd. . . $	75	-	85
Celery Vase	60	-	70
Comport, cvd., high . .	110	-	125
Creamer	45	-	50
Goblet	60	-	70
Nappy			20
Pickle Dish			25
Pitcher, water	100	-	110
Spooner	40	-	45
Sugar, cvd.	65	-	75
Wine	40	-	45

195

BUTTON ARCHES

Goblet, clear . . . . $	40	-	45
Goblet, ruby stained,			
Canadian place name	55	-	60
Nappy, clear			20
Toothpick, ruby stained.			20
Tumbler, milk glass,			
Canadian place name	40	-	45
Wine, clear	25	-	30

CANADIAN/CAPE COD

Bowl, cvd., diam. 6" $	130	-	150
Celery Vase	85	-	90
Comport, cvd., high . .	175	-	190
Comport, cvd., low . .	155	-	170
Creamer	85	-	95
Goblet, Canadian	140	-	145
Goblet, Cape Cod . .	85	-	100
Nappy, flat	25	-	30
Pitcher, milk	175	-	195
Plate, c.h., Diam. 8" . .	55	-	65
Spooner	65	-	75
Sugar, cvd.	125	-	140
Wine	70	-	80

BUTTONS & BOWS

Bowls, cvd. . . . . . . $	175	-	200
Comport, cvd., 6" . .	220	-	250
Goblet	125	-	135
Mustard	65	-	70
Nappy	30	-	35
Pitcher, water	300	-	335
Salt & Pepper			90
Sugar, cvd.	155	-	175

CANADIAN DRAPE

Butter Dish, cvd. . . $	85	-	95
Comport, cvd.	110	-	120
Creamer	60	-	70
Goblet	85	-	90
Nappy			20
Pitcher, chevron mark			140
Spooner	45	-	50

CANADIAN HORSESHOE

Bowl, diam. 9" . . $	25	-	30
Butter Dish, cvd.	60	-	70
Creamer	40	-	45
Creamer, individual . .	20	-	25
Custard Cup	20	-	25
Mug, Ht. 2¾"	20	-	25
Nappy			20
Spooner	30	-	35
Sugar, cvd.	60	-	65
Sugar, individual	25	-	30
Toothpick			20

CARDINAL

Butter Dish, cvd. . . $	115	-	125
Creamer	55	-	60
Goblet	80	-	95
Nappy, footed			25
Pitcher, water	95	-	110
Spooner	40	-	45
Sugar, cvd.	80	-	90

NOTE: Prices are for clear pieces, unless mentioned otherwise.
Coloured and opaque pieces usually bring higher prices.

CANADIAN THISTLE

Bowls . . . . $	40	-	60
Butter Dish, cvd.	100	-	115
Celery Vase	45	-	50
Creamer	50	-	55
Goblet	85	-	95
Honey Dish, cvd. 5"sq.	80	-	90
Nappy, flat			20
Nappy, footed	20	-	25
Oil/Vinegar Cruet . .	45	-	50
Pickle Dish			25
Pitcher, water	85	-	95
Salt, individual			20
Spooner	40	-	45
Sugar, cvd.	80	-	85

CAT'S EYE & FAN

Comport, cvd. . . . . $	80	-	90
Creamer	50	-	55
Goblet	70	-	80
Nappy, flat			20
Spooner	40	-	45

CENTENNIAL

Butter Dish, cvd. . .	$ 150	-	160
Cake Stand	70	-	80
Comport, open, Ht. 6½"	80	-	90
Creamer	95	-	105
Pitcher, water	115	-	125
Spooner	75	-	85

CHANDELIER

Bowl, diam. 8" . . $	105	-	115
Butter Dish, cvd.	150	-	165
Celery Vase	60	-	70
Creamer	105	-	115
Goblet	150	-	160
Nappy			30
Pitcher, water	175	-	195
Spooner	45	-	50
Sugar, cvd.	120	-	130

CHAIN WITH STAR

Butter Dish, cvd. . . $	65	-	70
Butter Dish, cvd. Ftd	80	-	85
Comport, cvd., high . .	90	-	95
Creamer	40	-	45
Goblet	50	-	55
Nappy, footed			15
Pitcher, water	80	-	85
Plate, handled	45	-	50
Spooner	35	-	40
Sugar, cvd.	75	-	80
Syrup	100	-	110
Wine			35

CLEAR DIAGONAL BAND

Bread Platter . . . . $	55	-	60
Butter Dish, cvd.	45	-	50
Celery Vase	30	-	35
Comport, cvd.	60	-	65
Goblet			40
Nappy			10
Spooner			25
Sugar, cvd.	35	-	40
Wine	30	-	35

CLEAR FUCHSIA

Butter Dish, cvd. . . $	70	-	80
Creamer	40	-	45
Goblet	75	-	80
Nappy			20
Relish Dish			25
Spooner			35

COLOSSUS

Bowl, diam. 8" .. $	30	-	35
Comport, cvd.	80	-	90
Creamer	40	-	45
Goblet	80	-	90
Pitcher, water	75	-	80
Spooner			30

COLONIAL

Banana Split Dish $			20
Butter Dish, cvd.	45	-	50
Butter Tub, cvd.	35	-	40
Cake Stand	25	-	30
Celery Vase	25	-	30
Comport, cvd.	45	-	50
Creamer, cvd.	45	-	50
Goblet			35
Nappy			10
Parfait			20
Pitcher, 3 pint	25	-	30
Salt, footed			15
Spooner	20	-	25
Sugar, cvd.	30	-	35

CONCORDIA MAPLE LEAF

Bread Plater - Wheat

Sheaf in centre $	80	-	90
Butter Dish, cvd.	200	-	225
Butter Pat, diam. 3"			35
Nappy			35
Plate, one central leaf	115	-	125
Plate, maple leaf flange	125	-	135
Relish Dish	40	-	45

CORD & TASSEL

Celery Vase	.... $ 60	-	65
Comport, cvd.	 100	-	110
Goblet	 70	-	80
Nappy	 20		
Pickle Dish	 30		
Wine	 60	-	65

NOTE: Prices are for clear pieces, unless mentioned otherwise.
Coloured and opaque pieces usually bring higher prices.

CROSS

Butter Dish, cvd.	... $ 70	-	80
Celery Vase	 45	-	50
Creamer	 40	-	45
Fruit Stand	 70	-	80
Goblet	 45	-	55
Nappy, handled, diam. 6"	 25		
Spooner	 35		
Sugar, cvd.	 50	-	55

COSMOS — Milk Glass

Butter Dish, cvd.	.. $ 300	-	325
Creamer	 200	-	225
Spooner	 175	-	200
Sugar, cvd.	 250	-	275
Syrup	 225	-	250

CROWN

Bon-Bon Dish	.... $ 160	-	175
Cake Stand (Hobnail)	225	-	250
Comport, cvd.	 325	-	350
Comport, open	 175	-	190
Creamer	 200	-	225
Gobelt	 350	-	395
Platter (Hobnail)	 150	-	175
Spooner	 105	-	115
Sugar, cvd.	 150	-	175
Tumbler	 185	-	200

CURLED LEAF

Creamer ...... $ 35 - 40
Goblet 50
Spooner 30

DAHLIA

Butter Dish, cvd. $ 65 - 70
Champagne .... 100 - 110
Cordial .... 75 - 85
Creamer 40
Goblet .... 85 - 95
Nappy, flat 15
Pitcher, water .... 70 - 75
Platter, oval 45
Relish Dish 20
Spooner 30
Sugar, cvd. ...... 55 - 60
Wine .... 60 - 65

NOTE: Prices are for clear pieces, unless mentioned otherwise.
Coloured and opaque pieces usually bring higher prices.

CURRANT

Comport, cvd. .. $ 100 - 110
Goblet .... 55 - 60
Pitcher, water ...... 90 - 95
Spooner .... 35 - 40
Wine 50

DAISY & BUTTON

Basket, 6" ...... $ 35 - 40
Creamer .... 25 - 30
Egg Cup 20
Goblet 50
Toothpick, hat shape 30 - 35
Tumbler 30

DAISY AND X BAND

Basket . . . . $	75	-	85
Butter Dish, cvd.	75	-	85
Celery Vase, handled	40	-	45
Child's four piece set	85	-	95
Comport, open, Ht. 6"	55	-	60
Goblet	325	-	350
Nappy, footed			25
Pitcher, water	80	-	90
Spooner			40
Sugar, cvd.	60	-	65
Wine			45

DAISY WITH PETTICOAT BAND

Bowl, open . . . . $	100	-	115
Butter Dish, cvd.	140	-	150
Cake Stand	140	-	150
Celery Vase	80	-	90
Comport, cvd.	175	-	195
Creamer	80	-	90
Goblet	350	-	395
Nappy			35
Pitcher, water	115	-	125
Spooner	60	-	65
Sugar, cvd.	115	-	125
Tankard	200	-	225

DAISY WITH THUMBPRINT

Butter Dish, cvd. . . $	70	-	75
Celery Vase	55	-	60
Creamer	55	-	60
Goblet	70	-	75
Nappy, flat			20
Spooner			45
Sugar, cvd.	60	-	65
Wine			40

DAISY WITH DEPRESSED BUTTON

Bowl, diam. 8½" . . $	40	-	45
Butter Dish, cvd.	70	-	75
Cake Stand	45	-	50
Creamer			45
Goblet	55	-	60
Nappy, flat			15
Nappy, footed			20
Spooner			35
Sugar, cvd.	60	-	65
Wine			40

DEER & DOG

Butter Dish, cvd. . . $ 200	-	225
Celery Vase 130	-	145
Comport, cvd. 200	-	225
Cordial 200	-	225
Creamer 115	-	125
Goblet 110	-	120
Jam Jar 185	-	200
Spooner 75	-	85
Sugar, cvd. 145	-	160
Wine 200	-	225

DIAGONAL BAND

Comport, cvd. . . $ 80	-	90
Goblet 50	-	55
Pitcher, water 75	-	85
Wine		35

DIAGONAL BAND & FAN

Champagne . . . $ 40	-	45
Comport, cvd. 80	-	90
Cordial		40
Goblet 45	-	50
Nappy		15
Spooner		30
Wine		35

DOG

Butter Dish, cvd. . . $ 115	-	125
Celery Vase 55	-	60
Comport, cvd. 165	-	175
Creamer 60	-	65
Spooner		45
Sugar, cvd. 115	-	125

DIAMOND

Butter Dish, cvd. . . $	160	-	175
Goblet	145	-	160
Nappy, flat			20
Nappy, footed			25
Sugar, cvd.	125	-	135

DIAMOND & SUNBURST

Bread Platter . . . . $	45	-	50
Comport, cvd. Ht. 9¼"	80	-	85
Egg Cup			35
Goblet	60	-	65
Nappy			20
Pitcher, water	115	-	125
Sugar, cvd.	65	-	70

NOTE: Prices are for clear pieces, unless mentioned otherwise.
Coloured and opaque pieces usually bring higher prices.

DIAMOND RAY

Bowl, diam. 9¼" . . $	115	-	125
Butter Dish, cvd.	140	-	150
Cake Stand	50	-	55
Comport, cvd.	100	-	110
Comport, cvd., global	140	-	150
Comport, open			45
Creamer	120	-	130
Goblet	125	-	135
Spooner	70	-	75
Sugar, cvd.	110	-	120

DIAMOND MEDALLION

Butter Dish, cvd. . . $	60	-	65
Cake Plate, diam. 10"	40	-	45
Cake Stand			40
Comport, cvd., high . .	70	-	75
Creamer			35
Goblet	65	-	70
Pitcher, water	70	-	75
Spooner			35
Sugar, cvd.	50	-	55
Wine	50	-	55

DOMINION

Butter Dish, cvd. . . $	85	-	90
Candy Jar,			
Footed, Ht. 13½"	105	-	115
Candy Jar, square . .	85	-	95
Celery Vase	60	-	65
Comport, cvd. large . .	110	-	120
Comport, open	75	-	85
Creamer	55	-	60
Goblet	85	-	95
Nappy, footed			25
Shaker, salt	25	-	30
Spooner	40	-	45
Sugar, cvd. ,	75	-	80
Wine			50

FAN BAND

Butter Dish, cvd. . . $	50	-	55
Celery Vase			40
Creamer			35
Goblet			40
Spooner			30
Sugar, cvd.			45
Wine			30

1883 PATTERN

Cake Stand . . . . . . $	65	-	70
Candy Dish, length 9"			50
Comport, cvd.	80	-	90
Creamer	55	-	60
Sugar, cvd.	70	-	80

FEATHER BAND

Butter Dish, cvd. . . $	60	-	65
Creamer			35
Pitcher, water	60	-	70
Plate, diam. 5½"			20
Spooner			30
Sugar, cvd.			50
Tumbler			35

ESTHER

Butter Dish, cvd. . . $	120	-	130
Creamer	70	-	75
Goblet	100	-	110
Pitcher, water	140	-	150
Spooner			50
Sugar, cvd.	100	-	110
Wine	65	-	75

FERN BURST

Butter Dish, cvd. . . $	45	-	50
Creamer			30
Goblet			45
Spooner			20
Sundae			15

FILLY

Butter Dish, cvd. . . $	85	-	95
Celery Vase	70	-	75
Creamer	60	-	65
Goblet			50
Spooner	50	-	55
Tumbler, footed			40
Wine			45

FLORAL - N.S.

Butter Dish, cvd. . . $	175	-	190
Creamer	100	-	110
Goblet	550	-	600
Jam Jar, glass lid	100	-	110
Pickle, single in silver			
plate stand	125	-	135
Pitcher, water	130	-	140
Spooner	75	-	85
Sugar, cvd.	140	-	150

FISHSCALE

Goblet .... $	50
Plate, diam. 9"	30
Salt, ftd., opaque blue	40

FLAT DIAMOND

Goblet .... $	40
Spooner	30
Sugar, cvd.	45
Wine	30

FLOWER & QUILL

Butter Dish, cvd. . . $	70	-	80
Celery Vase	60	-	65
Creamer	40	-	45
Nappy			20
Spooner	35	-	40

GOOD LUCK

Comport, cvd. .. $ 140	-	150
Creamer 40	-	45
Goblet 65	-	75
Goblet, knob stem .. 90	-	95
Pickle Dish		25
Platter 100	-	110
Wine 225	-	250

GOOSEBERRY

Creamer .... $ 55	-	60
Goblet 60	-	65
Nappy		20
Spooner 40	-	45

FROSTED FLOWER BAND

Butter Dish, cvd. .. $ 135	-	145
Comport, cvd., low .. 150	-	160
Goblet —		
With frosting 120	-	130
Without frosting .. 100	-	110
Nappy, footed		25
Pitcher, milk 80	-	90
Pitcher, water 90	-	100

NOTE: Prices are for clear pieces, unless mentioned otherwise.
Coloured and opaque pieces usually bring higher prices.

FROSTED RIBBON

Celery Vase .... $ 45	-	50
Egg Cup 35	-	40
Goblet 55	-	60
Nappy, flat		15
Relish Dish		20
Spooner 35	-	40

GESNER

Butter Dish, cvd. .. $ 55	-	60
Celery Vase 50	-	55
Creamer 45	-	50
Goblet 75	-	85
Salt, open		15
Spooner 35	-	40
Sugar, cvd. 60	-	65
	Etched pieces + 20%	

GRAPE & FESTOON WITH SHIELD

Creamer ..... $ 65	-	70
Goblet 70	-	75
Nappy		20
Mugs 30	-	40
Sugar, cvd. 80	-	85

HAMILTON

Comport, open . . $	60 -	65
Egg Cup	30 -	35
Goblet	60 -	65
Spooner	40 -	45
Tumbler	35 -	40
Wine	40 -	45

GRAPE & VINE - N.S.

Bowl, cvd., diam. 7" $	200 -	225
Butter Dish, cvd.	175 -	195
Cheese Bell	140 -	150
Comport, cvd.	170 -	185
Creamer	105 -	115
Goblet	120 -	135
Nappy, round		30
Pitcher, water	115 -	125
Plate, diam. 10¾" . .	100 -	110
Spooner	75 -	85
Sugar, cvd.	115 -	125

HONEYCOMB

Comport, cvd. . . . . . $	90 -	100
Creamer		35
Goblet		30
Nappy, footed		20
Wine		30

GREEK KEY & WEDDING RING

Butter Dish, cvd.,		
opalescent blue $	300 -	325
Celery,		
opalescent blue . .	275 -	300
Creamer,		
opalescent blue . .	175 -	200
Nappy,		
opalescent white		35
Spooner,		
opalescent blue . .	85 -	95
Syrup, opalescent blue,		
Britannia top	300 -	325
Tumbler,		
opalescent white . .	125 -	135

JEWEL BAND

Butter Dish, cvd. . . $	65 -	70
Bread Platter	50 -	60
Cake Stand	40 -	45
Comport, cvd.	80 -	90
Creamer	40 -	45
Goblet	40 -	45
Spooner	30 -	35
Sugar, cvd.	55 -	60
Wine		40

HOP'S BAND

Butter Dish, cvd. . . $	60 -	65
Egg Cup, large	35 -	40
Goblet		45
Relish Dish		25
Tumbler, footed	35 -	40
Wine	40 -	45

JUBILEE

Bowl, diam. 9½" . . $		25
Butter Dish, cvd.	55 -	60
Comport, cvd.	80 -	85
Creamer		30
Goblet	80 -	90
Spooner		30
Sugar, cvd.		50

NOTE: Prices are for clear pieces, unless mentioned otherwise.
Coloured and opaque pieces usually bring higher prices.

JACOB'S LADDER - EARLY

Bread Platter . . . . $	65 -	75
Butter Dish, cvd. . . .	100 -	110
Celery Vase	65 -	75
Comport, cvd.	125 -	135
Creamer	65 -	75
Goblet	110 -	120
Nappy, diam. 4½"		20
Pitcher, water	175 -	200
Relish Dish		25
Spooner	50 -	55
Sugar, cvd.	90 -	100
Wine	75 -	85

LATTICE

Butter Dish, cvd. . . $	60 -	70
Comport, cvd.	80 -	90
Creamer		45
Goblet	55 -	60
Nappy, flat		15
Spooner		35
Wine	40 -	45

LEAF & DART

Butter Dish, cvd. . . $	80	-	90
Creamer	45	-	50
Egg Cup	40	-	45
Goblet	55	-	60
Nappy, flat			20
Spooner	30	-	35
Sugar, cvd.	70	-	75
Wine	50	-	55

LEVERNE

Bowl, oval . . . . . . $			30
Butter Dish, cvd.	60	-	65
Celery Vase	50	-	55
Comport, cvd. Ht. 12¼''	100	-	110
Goblet	60	-	65
Nappy			15
Pitcher, water	80	-	90
Sugar, cvd.	70	-	80

LION

Bread Platter . . . . $	265	-	285
Comport, cvd., large, with frosting	275	-	325
Comport, cvd. oval, with frosting	250	-	275
Creamer	125	-	150
Pickle Dish	170	-	180
Spooner	90	-	100
Sugar, cvd.	160	-	175

LILY-OF-THE-VALLEY

Butter Dish, cvd. . . $	100	-	110
Celery Vase	75	-	85
Creamer	60	-	65
Goblet	110	-	120
Nappy	20	-	25
Pickle Dish			30
Pitcher, water	160	-	175
Sugar, cvd.	80	-	90

LOOP & PILLAR

Bowl, diam. 8½'' , . $	40	-	45
Butter Dish, cvd.	60	-	65
Creamer			40
Goblet	65	-	70
Spooner			35
Sugar, cvd.	45	-	50
Tumbler			35

LOOP & STAR

Bowl, diam. 8¼" . . $	30 -	35
Butter Dish, cvd.	55 -	60
Creamer	30 -	35
Pitcher, water	55 -	60
Plate, diam. 9¼"		30
Sugar, cvd.	45 -	50

LOZENGES

Comport, cvd.		
Ht. 13½" . . . . $	100 -	110
Comport, open, Ht. 7"		
ruffled edge	55 -	60
Nappy, ruffled edge		20

LOTUS WITH SERPENT

Butter Dish, cvd. . . $	120 -	130
Creamer	60 -	70
Goblet	155 -	165
Mug	40 -	45
Pitcher, water	170 -	180
Spooner	50 -	55
Sugar, cvd.	90 -	100

MAPLE LEAF

Bowl, open . . . . . . $	115 -	125
Butter Dish, cvd.	105 -	115
Cake Stand	70 -	75
Comport, open	75 -	85
Comport, open,		
ruffled	175 -	200
Creamer	65 -	75
Nappy		35
Pitcher, water	100 -	110
Spooner	60 -	70
Sugar, cvd.	85 -	95

MINERVA

Bread Platter	. . . . $	80	- 90
Bowl, footed	. . . . . .	45	- 50
Comport, cvd.	. . . . . .	135	- 145
Creamer	. . . .	75	- 85
Goblet	. . . .	135	- 150
Nappy	. . . .		25
Pitcher, water	. . . . . .	115	- 125
Spooner	. . . .	55	- 60

NEW CENTURY

Nappy, green with gold	. . . . $	15
Fruit Bowl, green with gold	. .	35
Fruit Bowl, green with gold in Toronto Silver Plate Company stand	. . . .	185
Spooner, clear with green	. . . .	35
Toothpick, clear	. . . .	15

NOTE: Prices are for clear pieces, unless mentioned otherwise.
Coloured and opaque pieces usually bring higher prices.

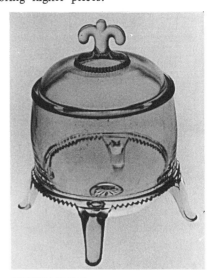

MONTREAL DIAMOND BAND

Bowl, cvd.	. . . . . . $	45	- 50
Butter Dish, cvd.	. . . .	60	- 65
Comport, open	. . . .	40	- 45
Creamer	. . . .		35
Goblet	. . . .	55	- 60
Nappy, footed	. . . .		15
Pitcher, water	. . . . . .	70	- 80
Spooner	. . . .		30
Sugar, cvd.	. . . .	45	- 50

NEWCASTLE

Comport, cvd., Ht. 8"	. . . . $	175
Creamer	. . . .	60
Salt, open	. . . .	20
Spooner	. . . .	50
Sugar, cvd.	. . . .	90

212

NUGGET - EARLY

Butter Dish, cvd. . . $	80	-	90
Comport, open	65	-	70
Creamer	50	-	55
Nappy			20
Pitcher, water	65	-	70
Pitcher, water, green	200	-	225
Spooner	40	-	45
Tumbler			40
Water Tray	60	-	70

ONE-O-ONE

Bread Platter . . . . $	80	-	90
Butter Dish, cvd.	80	-	85
Celery Vase	60	-	65
Comport, cvd.	115	-	125
Creamer	40	-	45
Goblet	85	-	95
Nappy			20
Spooner			35
Sugar, cvd.	70	-	75

NUGGET - LATE

Butter Dish, cvd. . . $	70	-	80
Cake Stand	55	-	60
Comport, cvd.	65	-	70
Creamer	40	-	45
Nappy			15
Pitcher, water	65	-	70
Spooner	40	-	45
Sugar, cvd.	70	-	75
Tumbler	35	-	40

PALING - BANDED

Creamer . . . . . . $	40	-	45
Goblet	50	-	55

PALING - PLAIN

Goblet . . . . $	40	-	45

PALMETTE

Butter Dish, cvd. . . $	80	-	90
Celery Dish	75	-	80
Comport, open	80	-	90
Creamer	70	-	75
Goblet	70	-	75
Nappy			20
Salt, footed	35	-	40
Shakers, clear, pair . .	55	-	60
Shakers, opaque, pair	90	-	100
Spooner	40	-	45
Sugar, cvd.	80	-	85
Wine	115	-	125

PANELLED DEWDROP

Bowl, oval . . . . $		30
Bread Platter		60
Celery Vase		40
Creamer		35
Goblet		50
Wine		40

PANELLED FORGET-ME-NOT

Butter Dish, cvd. . . $	90	-	95
Cake Stand, large . .	55	-	60
Cake Stand, small . .	50	-	55
Celery Vase	70	-	75
Comport, cvd.	110	-	120
Creamer	55	-	60
Goblet	75	-	80
Pickle Dish			25
Pitcher, water	85	-	95
Spooner	45	-	50
Sugar, cvd.	70	-	75

PANELLED CANE

Creamer . . . . $	40
Goblet	45
Nappy	15
Spooner	30

PEERLESS

Celery Vase . . . . $	55	-	60
Comport, cvd., Ht. 9"	90	-	100
Egg Cup	30	-	35
Goblet	55	-	60
Nappy			15
Tumbler	35	-	40
Wine	35	-	40

PERSIAN SPEAR

Comport, cvd., Ht. 8¼" . . . . . . $	105	-	115
Creamer	55	-	60
Decanter, original stopper			175
Goblet	65	-	70
Sugar, open		.	40

PEQUOT

Bowl, ftd., diam. 8" $	55	-	60
Butter Dish, cvd.	80	-	90
Creamer	60	-	65
Goblet	70	-	75
Sugar, cvd.	70	-	75

PICKET

Bread Platter . . . . $	60	-	65
Butter Dish, cvd.	70	-	75
Celery Vase	60	-	65
Comport, open, Ht. 5½"	40	-	45
Goblet	70	-	80
Nappy			15
Spooner	35	-	40

PLEAT & PANEL

Bowl, open . . . . . . $		35
Bowl, footed, covered,		
Ht. 5¼"	55 -	60
Butter Dish, cvd.	65 -	70
Cake Stand	55 -	60
Creamer	40 -	45
Goblet	55 -	60
Salt, master		25
Spooner		35
Sugar, cvd.		55

PILLOW ENCIRCLED

Butter Dish, cvd. . . $	60 -	65
Comport, open, Ht. 7¾"	50 -	55
Nappy		15
Sugar, cvd.	55 -	60
Tankard	85 -	95
Tumbler	30 -	35

NOTE: Prices are for clear pieces, unless mentioned otherwise.
Coloured and opaque pieces usually bring higher prices.

PITCAIRN

Butter Dish, cvd. . . $	65 -	75
Creamer		40
Egg Cup	30 -	35
Goblet	60 -	65
Nappy, flat		15
Spooner		40
Sugar, cvd.		60

POINTED BULLSEYE

Banana Dish . . . . $	175 -	200
Bowl, fruit, diam. 10¼"	115 -	125
Butter Dish, cvd.	95 -	105
Celery Vase	80 -	85
Creamer	70 -	75
Goblet	165 -	175
Nappy, diam. 3¾"		30
Pitcher, water	150 -	165
Spooner	60 -	65
Sugar, cvd.	85 -	90
Tumbler	60 -	65

QUEEN VICTORIA COMMEMORATIVE

Butter Dish, cvd., Golden
   Jubilee 1837 - 1887 . . . . $ 195
Creamer, Diamond Jubilee
   1837 - 1897 140
Creamer, Golden Jubilee
   1837 - 1887 140
Nappy, skirted 25
Plate, single head surrounded by
   wreath, with date 1837 80
Plate, single head surrounded by
   sunburst medallion 80
Plate, double head surrounded
   by wreath, date 1837 110
Plate, double head surrounded
   by sunburst medallion 110
Spooner, Golden Jubilee
   1837 - 1887 100

RASPBERRY & SHIELD

Butter Dish, cvd. . . $ 165 - 175
Creamer . . . . 115 - 125
Goblet . . . . 155 - 165
Jam/Marmalade . . . . 115 - 125
Pickle in Standard Silver
   Co., frame 195
Sugar, cvd. . . . . 135 - 145
Spooner . . . . 85 - 95

RAYED HEART

Bowl, diam. 8" . . $ 60 - 65
Butter Dish, cvd. . . . . 125 - 135
Celery Dish, flat . . . . 75 - 80
Creamer . . . . 75 - 80
Goblet* . . . . 950 - 1000
Jelly Comport, opalescent 700
Nappy 30
Spooner . . . . 70 - 75
Sugar, cvd. . . . . 90 - 95
Tumbler . . . . 65 - 70
*See following page

RASPBERRY

Goblet . . . . $ 140 - 150
Nappy 30
Plate, diam. 7" . . . . 55 - 60
Plate, diam. 10" . . . . 50 - 55
Plate, diam. 11¼" . . 50 - 55

RAYED HEART

Reproduced Goblet.
Set of 4, issued in 1982
by Canadian Collector Plates,
sold for $100

*NOTE: Goblet reproduced, recessed
Logo or mark of Canadian Collector
Plates Limited, Milliken, Ontario on
base of each goblet.*

*Left —
Logo of Canadian
Collector Plates
Limited.*

*From: Canadian Handbook of Pressed
Glass Tableware.
By: Peter Unitt and Anne Worrall.*

NOTE: Prices are for clear pieces,
unless mentioned otherwise.
Coloured and opaque pieces usually
bring higher prices.

RIBBON & STAR

Butter Dish, cvd. . . $.	155 -	165
Comport, cvd., Ht. 8"	175 -	190
Creamer	105 -	115
Goblet	100 -	115
Jam/Marmalade	120 -	130
Nappy		25
Salt, master		30
Spooner	70 -	80
Sugar, cvd.	130 -	140
Tumbler	55 -	60

RIBBED BAND

Bowl, cvd., diam. 6" $	115 -	125
Butter Dish, cvd.	140 -	150
Comport, Ht. 7¼" . .	100 -	110
Creamer	80 -	90
Goblet	100 -	110
Nappy		25
Pitcher, water	80 -	90
Spooner	60 -	65
Sugar, cvd.	85 -	95

SAWTOOTH

Butter Dish, cvd. . . $.	60 -	65
Creamer	45 -	50
Goblet	50 -	55
Nappy		15
Spooner	30 -	35
Toothpick, hat shape		20
Wine	35 -	40

SCALLOPED LINES

Comport, cvd.	. . $	85 -	90
Comport, open	. . . .	65 -	70
Creamer	. . . .	50 -	55
Egg Cup	. . . .	30 -	35
Goblet	. . . .	50 -	55
Wine		45 -	50

SENECA LOOP

Comport, cvd. . . . . $	100 -	110
Creamer	. . . .	50 -	55
Goblet	. . . .	45 -	50
Spooner	. . . .	35 -	40

SHERATON

Bread Platter	. . . . $	45 -	50
Butter Dish, cvd.	. . . .	65 -	70
Comport, cvd.	. . . .	85 -	95
Creamer	. . . .	40 -	45
Goblet	. . . .	55 -	60
Pitcher, water	. . . . . .	70 -	75
Spooner	. . . .		35
Sugar, cvd.	. . . .	60 -	65
Wine			45

SHELL & TASSEL

Butter Dish, cvd	. . $	105 -	115
Cake Stand	. . . . . .	55 -	60
Celery Vase, handled		65 -	70
Creamer	. . . .	60 -	65
Goblet	. . . .	80 -	85
Nappy	. . . .			20

SQUARE MARSH PINK

Butter Dish, cvd.	. . $	100 -	110
Creamer	. . . .	70 -	75
Jam/Marmalade	. . . .	85 -	95
Nappy, ftd, 4" x 4"	. . . .		25
Pickle Dish			35
Plate	45 -	50
Spooner	. . . .	55 -	60

STARFLOWER

Butter Dish, cvd.	. . . $	200	-	225
Cake Stand	. . . . . .	45	-	50
Creamer	. . . .	115	-	125
Comport, cvd., plain foot & stem	. . . .	125	-	135
Comport, open, ornate stem, fluted foot	. .	130	-	140
Goblet	. . . .	150	-	170
Nappy, dewdrop base	. . . . . .			25
Pitcher, milk	. . . . . .	105	-	115
Pitcher, water	. . . . . .	90	-	100
Spooner	. . . .	75	-	80
Sugar, cvd.	. . . .	100	-	110

NOTE: Prices are for clear pieces, unless mentioned otherwise.
Coloured and opaque pieces usually bring higher prices.

STIPPLED SWIRL & STAR

Bowl, diam. 8"	. . $	30	-	35
Butter Dish, cvd.	. . . .	60	-	65
Comport, cvd.	. . . .	85	-	95
Creamer	. . . .	35	-	40
Nappy	. . . .			15
Pitcher, water	. . . . . .	65	-	70
Spooner	. . . .			35
Sugar, cvd.	. . . .	55	-	60

STRAWBERRY

Creamer	. . . . . . $	50	-	55
Goblet	. . . .	65	-	70
Pickle Dish	. . . .			25
Spooner	. . . .	35	-	40
Sugar, cvd.	. . . .	75	-	80

SUNBURST

Goblet	. . . . $		40
Spooner	. . . .		35
Wine	. . . .		40

SUNBURST MEDALLION

Creamer	. . . . $		35
Goblet	. . . .		65
Nappy	. . . .		10
Spooner	. . . .		35
Wine	. . . .		55

SUNKEN BULLSEYE

Butter Dish, cvd. . . $	80	-	90
Comport, open	70	-	75
Creamer	65	-	70
Goblet	105	-	115
Pitcher, water	90	-	100
Salt Shaker	35	-	40
Spooner	40	-	45
Wine	60	-	65

TASSEL & CREST - N.S.

Butter Dish, cvd. . . $	100	-	110
Comport, cvd.	140	-	155
Creamer	75	-	85
Nappy, ftd.			25
Spooner	55	-	60
Sugar, cvd.	80	-	90

THISTLE

Comport, cvd. ht. 9" $	100	-	110
Goblet	75	-	85
Nappy			15
Spooner	40	-	45
Relish Dish			25
Wine	55	-	60

TANDEM - N.S.

Celery Vase .... $	125	-	135
Goblet	90	-	100
Plate, diam. 6"	40	-	45
Plate, diam. 10"	45	-	50

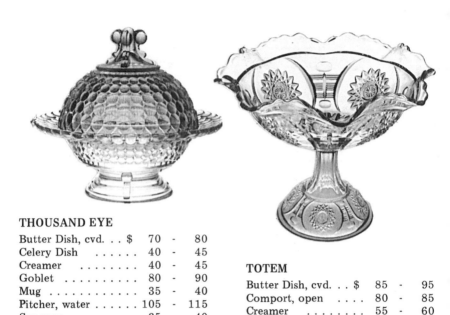

THOUSAND EYE

Butter Dish, cvd. . . $	70 -	80
Celery Dish	40 -	45
Creamer	40 -	45
Goblet	80 -	90
Mug	35 -	40
Pitcher, water	105 -	115
Spooner	35 -	40
Sugar, cvd.	65 -	75
Toothpick		20
Tumbler	30 -	35

TOTEM

Butter Dish, cvd. . . $	85 -	95
Comport, open	80 -	85
Creamer	55 -	60
Spooner	40 -	45
Sugar, cvd.	70 -	80

THREE PANEL

Butter Dish, cvd. . . $	65 -	75
Cracker Bowl	40 -	45
Creamer	45 -	50
Goblet	50 -	55
Nappy		15
Pitcher, water	65 -	70
Spooner	35 -	40
Sugar, cvd.	60 -	65
Tumbler	25 -	30

TREE OF LIFE

Bowl, diam. 6¼'' . . $	30 -	35
Goblet	90 -	100
Pitcher, water	65 -	70

TRENTON BLOCK

Butter Dish, cvd. . . . $ 165	-	180
Goblet 350		395
Sugar, cvd. 140	-	150
Tumbler 90	-	100

UTAH

Pitcher, water . . . . $ 40 -   45

TULIP WITH SAWTOOTH

Celery Vase . . . . $ 70	-	80
Comport, cvd. ht.13¼" 145	-	160
Egg Cup 40	-	45
Goblet 60	-	65
Salt, master 40	-	45
Spooner 45	-	50
Wine 45	-	50

WASHINGTON CENTENNIAL

Bowl, diam. 7" . . $ 35	-	40
Celery Vase 60	-	70
Creamer 40	-	45
Goblet 75	-	80

WESTWARD HO

Butter Dish, cvd. . . $			375
Celery Dish			150

Butter Dish, cvd. . . $	350	-	375
Celery Dish	135	-	150
Comport, cvd., oval,			
Ht. 10½"	290	-	325
Comport, cvd.Ht.11¼"	250	-	300
Creamer	140	-	150
Goblet			225
Nappy, diam. 4½"			40
Sugar, cvd.			250

GOBLET PATTERNS — That do not come in sets of tableware.

BEAVER BAND . . $	800	-	1000
BOLING			40
CHAIN & STAR			
BAND	110	-	120
CLEAR & DIAMOND			
PANELS	70	-	80
EASTERN STAR . .	50	-	55
GOTHIC, N.S.	110	-	120
GRADUATED			
DIAMONDS	45	-	50
KENLEE, N.S.	115	-	125
PANELLED			
DIAMONDS	50	-	55
ST. JOHN'S —	Plain 60	-	65
	Etched 65	-	70
WAY'S CURRANT . .	50	-	55

WOODROW

Biscuit/Candy Jar $	200	-	225
Butter Dish, cvd.	115	-	125
Cake Stand	105	-	115
Comport, open, Ht. 8"	80	-	90
Creamer	55	-	60
Custard Cup			25
Goblet	175	-	190
Nappy			20
Pitcher, water	110	-	120
Pitcher, with ice lip . .	165	-	185
Sundae Dish	25	-	30
Spooner	45	-	50
Sugar, cvd.	75	-	85
Toothpick			25
Tumbler	55	-	60
Water Carafe, Ht. 9"	175	-	190
Wine	80	-	90

NOTE: Prices are for clear pieces, unless mentioned otherwise.
Coloured and opaque pieces usually bring higher prices.

LIGHTING

LAMPS
Railway
Street
Hurricane etc

RAILWAY LAMP. Embossed
C.P.R. by Piper, Montreal.
Bullseye lenses.
Ht. 19½" $175.00

RAILWAY LAMP.
Bullseye lenses.
Ht. 16" $185.00

225

RAILROAD CONDUCTOR
or guard's lamp. Heavy sheet
metal, brass top and handle,
clear, green and red lenses.
Ht. 10½" $180.00

PORTABLE LAMP. Brass and
copper. Used by railway guards
or police etc. Late 1800's.
Ht. 12½" $195.00

BICYCLE LAMP. Acetelyne
fueled. Nickel plated. Ca. 1920.
Ht. 7¼" $85.00

"LAMPE PIGEON"
French, 1880's. $110.00

STATION/STREET LAMP.
Hurricane/windproof type.
Ca. 1880's. $150.00

HURRICANE/WINDPROOF
LAMP. Embossed "Ontario
Lantern." $25.00

"DEITZ" HAND LANTERN. Used
to light and signal, coloured
globe. $75.00

RAILROAD LAMP. Tin, in original
green painted condition. Marked
G.T.R. (Grand Trunk Railroad)
Ht. 17" $100.00

TIN WALL LAMP. Ca. 1910.
Wall mount 11" high. . . $40.00

HAND LAMP. Tin, painted black.
Ht. to top of collar 3" . . $40.00

HOLLAND BAKERS LAMP. Tin
stand or wall hung.
Ht. 9½" $85.00

SKATERS LAMP. Brass with tin
wire handle. Embossed on chimney
"Little Bobs"
Lamp 6¼" high $45.00

228

Christmas Tree Lights

CHRISTMAS TREE LIGHTS — 1930's. Measurements, 2½" to 3"
Top — Grapes, decorated purple and gold on silver. Each $12.50
Bottom — Left — Green grapes. 12.50
Bottom — Right — Lantern, purple and blue on silver 25.00

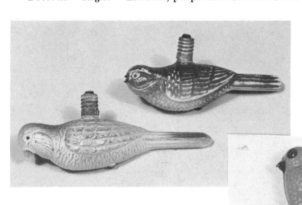

CHRISTMAS TREE LIGHTS —
Above — Budgies, 1930's.
L. 4" Each $30.00

Right — Birds, 1940's.
L. 3¼" Each 7.50

MILK GLASS CHRISTMAS TREE LIGHTS. Remnants of paint remaining.
Left to Right — Snowman — $25.00; Cottage — $17.50 —
Polar Bear with banjo — $30.00.   Measurements, about 3"

CHRISTMAS TREE LIGHTS. Disney characters, late 1930's.
Measurements, about 4"   Each $35.00

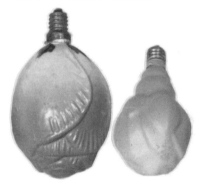

MILK GLASS SANTAS.
Left — 3¾"   . . $50.00
Right — 3" 35.00

TULIPS.
Left — 3½"   . . $40.00
Right — 2½"   . . 20.00

METALWARE

BRASS BELLS. British. Ht. 3" Left to Right —
Hoop Skirt Lady, Welsh Lady, Colonial Lady.
Each $25.00   - $30.00

Above —
BRASS BELLS. British, 1920's.
Left to Right —
Court Lady, Ht. 4" . . $35.00
Court Lady, Ht. 3" . .   35.00
Hoop Skirt Lady,
Ht. 4¾" 40.00

Right —
BRASS BELLS. 1920's.
Left — English Char
Lady. Ht. 4" $40.00
Right — Fiddler.
Ht. 5" 75.00

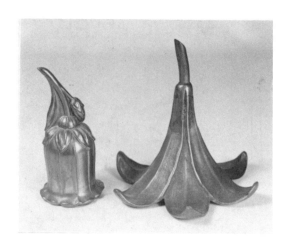

BRASS BELLS. 1920's.
Left — Canterbury Bell. Copy of the 14th century original.
Ht. 4" $80.00
Right — Lilly. 55.00

BRASS BELLS. 1930's.
Left — Sailing ship "Revenge"
Ht. 4" $20.00
Right — British Lamp Post.
Reg. No. 926811.
Ht. 7" 45.00

BRASS BELL. Engraved
"Joseph Cherpaw Bakery,
Uxbridge, Ont. 1898"
Marked J2 on top of casting.
Ht. 11½" $150.00

ART DECO FIGURES. Gilded composition athletes on alabaster stands. Ca. 1930's.
Ht. 10" Pair $1250.00

"THE CAT'S MEOW" Bronze Art Noveau lamp, 1906 - 10. Eyes light up when lamp is lit.
Ht. 14½" $750.00

Right —
BRASS PEN TRAY & INK WELLS. Art Nouveau, turtle covers on ink wells, peacock feather design on tray. Ca. 1910 - 15.
L. 12" . . $95.00

Left —
BRONZE CAMEL. Made to hold cigarette pack, origin unknown. Ca. 1920.
L. 4" . . $95.00

EVEN BALANCE SCALE.
Brass, wood base. 1890's.
Ht. 22" $195.00

COPPER URN. Brass tap, wood
knob on lid. Early 1900's.
Ht. 17" Diam. 12" . . $185.00

Left & Right —
MILK SHAKE BEAKERS. Coppered lips and bases.
Ht. 6"   Each $65.00
Centre —
SHAKER. With hinged strainer. 35.00

APPLE/GRAPE PRESS.
Sold by T. Eaton Co., early
1900's.
Frame 18" x 14" $495.00

DRILL PRESS/BORING MACHINE.
Used to drill holes in large timbers,
also used to cut mortises.
Length of base 29"
Ht. 23" $130.00

TOOL BOX. Pine, metal strapping
and fittings.
23" x 15" x 12" $125.00

WROUGHT IRON
HARPOON HEAD.
L. 9"   . . $25.00

RADIOS

Band: a range of broadcasting frequencies or wave lengths.

AM Band: (Amplitude Modulation) altering the amplitude of the transmitting radio wave in accordance with the signal being broadcast.

SW Band: (Short Wave) a radio wave with a length of eighty meters or less.

AC: (Alternating Current) electric current that reverses its direction at regular intervals.

DC: (Direct Current) power source supplied by battery, electric current flows in one direction.

PHILCO. Model 95B, 1937, AM. Battery only. Wood case. 14½" x 12" x 8" $150.00

HALLICRAFTERS. Portable AC/DC. 1952, AM, SW, 6 bands. "World Wide" radio in brown leatherette case. Fold down cover with map of the world. 12" x 18" x 8" $150.00

Left —
PHILCO. Portable, AC/DC.
1946, AM.
Wood case with roll top cover
over dial and controls, leather
handle.
12" x 9½" x 5" $95.00

Right —
MARCONI. Model 227, mid
1930's. AM. Battery only.
Plastic case.
7" x 9" x 5" $60.00

Left —
SENTINAL, Model 335, 1946,
AM. Portable, AC/DC.
Mottled cream plastic case with
handle.
7" x 9" x 5" $60.00

Right —
RCA VICTOR. Portable, battery
only, 1941. AM. Black leatherette
carrying case with chromed front.
ON/OFF switch activated by
hinges.
9" x 4" x 3" $50.00

Wednesday is Bingday

Listen to Bing Crosby on Philco Radio Time, his one and only radio program.

Every Wednesday at 10 P.M. in the East, 9 P.M. everywhere else. ABC Network and many additional stations.

Bing Crosby, star of Philco Radio Time enjoying the sensational Philco 1201.

The amzing new way to play records, invented by Philco. You just slide a record in and it plays automatically...no lid to lift, no tone arm to set, no bother with controls or needles. An overnight sensation...the largest selling radio-phonograph in the world. Available now at your Philco dealer.

PHILCO *Famous for Quality the World Over*

ADVERTISEMENT
Philco Radio-Phonograph Model 1201.

PHILCO. Model 1201, 1946. AM. Radio-phonograph combination in all wood case with gold coloured cloth speaker cover. Record is loaded through slot in lower compartment, a mechanism locates it and the tone arm moves into place.
11" x 16" x 15" $175.00

ADMIRAL. Combination, Late 1940's. AM. Radio-phonograph. Automatic record changer holds eight records, 78, 45 and 33 rpm. Maroon plastic case, buff coloured cloth speaker cover.
Closed 10" x 15" x 15" $111.00

238

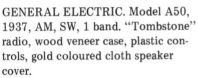

GENERAL ELECTRIC. Model A50, 1937, AM, SW, 1 band. "Tombstone" radio, wood veneer case, plastic controls, gold coloured cloth speaker cover.
16" x 13" x 9½" $175.00

ROGERS. Model R561, 1932, AM. Cathedral style radio, wood case, gold coloured cloth speaker cover.
16" x 12" x 8" $275.00

CANADIAN GENERAL ELECTRIC. Model JK53, 1942, AM, SW, 2 bands. Wood veneer case, cloth speaker grille.
13" x 14" x 9" $150.00

ADDISON. Model R583, Ca. 1947, AM. Solid wood case, gold colour cloth speaker cover.
9" x 13" x 7" $250.00

Above — Left —
PHILCO. Model 44B, 1934, AM,
SW, 2 bands.
"Beehive" radio with wood veneer
case and gold coloured cloth speaker cover.
18½" x 16" x 10" $250.00
Above — Right —
PHILCO. Model 20, 1929, AM.
"Beehive" radio, walnut veneer
case.
17½" x 16" x 10" 300.00

CANADIAN GENERAL ELECTRIC.
Radiola 18, 1927, AM.
Mahogany box case radio with lid,
separate speaker in wood veneer case.
Radio 9" x 27" x 8"
Speaker 12" x 10½" x 6½" $275.00

Right —
RCA. 1929, AM. Radio in dark brown
metal case with matching speaker.
Same type chassis as GE
Radiola 18. Speaker with
sunburst pattern cloth
grille.
Radio 9" x 27" x 8"
Speaker
10" x 11" x 5"$300.00

GENERAL ELECTRIC. Model 22, 1931, AM. "Tombstone" radio, walnut veneer case, cloth with needlepoint speaker panel.
19" x 14" x 10" $250.00

ELECTROHOME.
Model PMU51 - 488, Ca. 1951, AM. Picture radio with wood case, cloth speaker cover with petit point style flowers.
7½" x 10" x 5" $150.00

MARCONI. Model 144, 1938.
AM, SW, 2 bands. Console radio, wood veneer case, push button and electric eye tuning.
43" x 25" x 13" $250.00

CANADIAN WESTINGHOUSE.
Model 195, 1933, AM, SW, 1 band. Console radio, wood veneer case, electric eye tuning. Illuminated drawer under controls with list of frequencies.
42" x 23" x 13" $250.00

PHILCO. Model 121 44A, Early 1940's, AM, SW, 3 bands. Wood art deco style case, push button, fold down dial cover. 36" x 36" x 16" $225.00

ELECTROHOME. 1947, AM, SW, 1 band. Console radio, mixed wood veneer case. 31" x 28" x 12"   .. $120.00

GENERAL ELECTRIC LOW BOY. Model RC15, Ca. 1932, AM. Console radio, wood case, pressed wood front. 35" x 20" x 12" $400.00

GENERAL ELECTRIC. Model M55. 1932, AM. Console radio, all wood case. 38" x 21" x 15" $300.00

Left —
ELECTROHOME.
Model 650, 1936,
AM, SW, 1 band.
"Serenader" radio with
wood case and cloth
speaker grille.
10" x 19" x 8" $150.00

Right —
NORTHERN ELECTRIC.
Model 52A, 1934,
AM, SW, 1 band.
Art deco style mixed wood
veneer case, sun ray pattern
speaker grille with gold coloured cloth speaker cover.
11" x 15" x 8"   . . $350.00

Left —
STEWART - WARNER,
Model R186, 1935,
AM, SW, 2 bands.
Wood veneer case, brown
cloth grille, wood knobs.
12" x 17" x 9" $175.00

Right —
ROGERS - MAJESTIC.
Model 6M412, 1938, AM.
Wood case, black dial, gold
coloured cloth speaker grille.
8" x 10" x 5½"   . . $90.00

Left —
CANADIAN GENERAL
ELECTRIC. Model JK - 70,
1940, AM, SW, 5 bands.
Wood veneer case, push
buttons.
12½" x 22" x 10" $150.00

Right —
RCA, Model M46, 1946,
AM, SW, 3 bands.
Wood veneer case, push
buttons.
13" x 16" x 9"   . . $90.00

Left —
PHILCO. Model 475,
1940's. AM.
Wood case, gold coloured
cloth speaker grille.
8" x 13" x 7"
Excellent condition $100.00

Right —
WESTINGHOUSE.
Early 1940's, AM, SW,
1 band.
Mixed wood veneer case,
gold coloured cloth speaker
grille.
9" x 13½" x 7" . . $100.00

Left —
ROGERS - MAJESTIC.
Model R166, Late 1930's.
AM. Wood veneer case with
gold coloured cloth speaker
grille.
9" x 13" x 7" $100.00

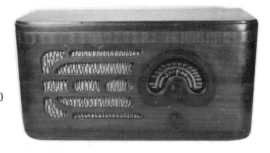

Right —
"SPARTON" Model 848.
Ca. 1940. AM.
Wood veneer case.
9" x 18" x 7½" . . $100.00

Left —
STROMBERG - CARLSON,
Canada. Model PA42, Ca. 1940.
AM. Book end radio, veneer
case.
8½" x 16" x 8" $200.00

Right —
BRAND & MILLAN.
Model DR102U, Ca. 1947.
AM. Astra radio with wood
veneer case.
9½" x 12" x 7" . . $125.00

CANADIAN GENERAL ELECTRIC.
1939, AM and Police.
Brown coloured wood case, push buttons.
10" x 14½" x 7" $75.00

This licence MUST be kept available for Inspection

This licence MUST be kept available for Inspection

(seal)
Canada   DEPARTMENT OF MARINE-RADIO BRANCH
                        1936-37

Private Radio Receiving Licence
(Issued under the Radiotelegraph Act, Revised Statutes of Canada,
1927, chapter 195)

(name)
IS HEREBY LICENCED, SUBJECT TO THE CONDITIONS SET FORTH ON
THE BACK HEREOF, TO ESTABLISH OR WORK A PRIVATE RADIO REC-
EIVING STATION AT —

(address)
AND IN ADDITION TO WORK ONE RADIO RECEIVING SET IN A PASSEN-
GER AUTOMOBILE OWNED BY THE LICENSEE.

THIS LICENCE EXPIRES ON THE 31ST MARCH, 1937

RECEIVED THE SUM OF TWO DOLLARS ($2.00) LICENCE FEE THIS 28th
                                        DAY OF NOV. A.D. 1936

ISSUED ON BEHALF OF THE MINISTER OF MARINE   (signature)

Right —
SENTINEL.
Model 286PR, 1948, AM.
AC/DC radio in red and
black plastic case with
handle. ON/OFF switch
activated by lid. $60.00

Left —
EMERSON. Model U5A,
1935, AM, SW, 1 band.
Brown plastic case, gold
coloured cloth speaker
grille.
10" x 7" x 5" . . $300.00

Right —
MONARCH. Model 102,
Late 1940's, AM. Made
in Montreal, Quebec.
Brown plastic case.
7" x 9½" x 6" $60.00

Left —
MOTOROLA. Model 55X11-A,
Late 1940's. AM.
Dark brown plastic case with
handle.
7" x 10" x 6" $70.00

Left —
ARVIN. Model 544AR,
Late 1940's, AM.
Cream painted plastic case.
6½" x 9½" x 5½"   . . $90.00

Right —
CANADIAN MARCONI.
Model 290, Early 1950's, AM.
Cream plastic case, brown metal
grille.
8" x 12" x 7" $80.00

Left —
CANADIAN GENERAL
ELECTRIC. Model C401
Ca. 1949, AM.
Mottled blue/green plastic
case, red control knobs.
5½" x 10" x 5½" $250.00

Right —
ROGERS - MAJESTIC.
Model RM502, Early 1950's.
AM. Plastic case painted pale
green.
7½" x 11" x 6" $65.00

Left —
GENERAL ELECTRIC.
Model C600, 1950, AM.
Brown plastic case with
gold speaker grille.
8¼" x 12" x 7" $60.00

Right —
GENERAL ELECTRIC.
Model C409, 1952, AM.
Brown plastic case with
plastic speaker grille.
10" x 14" x 8"   . . $70.00

Left —
CROSLEY.
Model 11-108U, Early 1950's.
AM. Maroon plastic case, gold
station scale and indicator.
10" x 12½" x 7" . . $75.00

Right —
NORTHERN ELECTRIC
TELECOM. Model 5800,
Early 1950's, AM.
"Baby Champ" radio with
two-tone green plastic case
gold numerals and station
indicator.
7½" x 13" x 7"   . . $80.00

RCA VICTOR —
Left — "Master Nipper" Ca. 1940. AM. Brown plastic case.
7" x 9" x 5" $80.00
Right — "Baby Nipper" Ca. 1940, AM. Brown plastic case.
5" x 8½" x 4½" 80.00
Both also can be found in cream coloured cases.

Left —
STEWART - WARNER.
Model R435, 1940, AM.
Dark brown plastic case,
white controls.
5½" x 10" x 5" $100.00

Right —
CANADIAN GENERAL
ELECTRIC. Model C453.
Early 1950's. AM.
Mottled plastic case.
9" x 12" x 8" . . $80.00

Right —
STROMBERG - CARLSON.
Model 561, Late 1940's.
AM. Dark brown plastic
case, gold coloured cloth
speaker grille.
8" x 13" x 8" . . $65.00

Left —
STEWART-WARNER.
Model R-193, Late 1930's.
AM. Battery radio in wood
veneer case, gold coloured
cloth speaker grille.
9" x 15" x 8" $80.00

Right —
NORTHERN ELECTRIC.
Model 414A, Mid 1930's.
AM. Wood veneer case,
gold coloured cloth
speaker grille.
7" x 11" x 6" $100.00

Left —
GENERAL ELECTRIC.
Model F52A, 1938,
AM and SW, 1 band.
With teledyne tuning
dial.
Wood veneer case, gold
coloured cloth speaker
grille.
9½" x 18" x 8" $175.00

Right —
PHILCO. Model TH-15,
Ca. 1940, AM.
"Transitone" radio with
wood veneer case, plastic
handle and knobs.
7" x 10" x 6" . . $100.00

JUKEBOXES

Left —
WURLITZER 61.
1938/39.
Table model.
78, 12 records,
12 selections. $5000.00

Values are for machines as new and in working order.
Machines in fair condition ½ value.
Machines in poor condition ¼ value.

Right —
WURLITZER 1015. 1946/47.
78, 24 records, 24 selections.
. . . . $15,000.00

WURLITZER 1100. 1948.
78, 24 records, 24 selections.
First jukebox with Zenith cobra
tonearm. $8900.00

WURLITZER 1400. 1951/52.
33 1/3, 45, 78, 48 selections.
. . . . $5000.00

WURLITZER 1450. 1951/52.
33 1/3, 45, 78, 24 records,
48 selections. $5500.00

WURLITZER 2810. 1964. Scarce.
45, 50 records, 100 selections.
. . . . $2700.00

NOT SHOWN —
SEEBURG Vogue. 1939.
78, 20 selections. $1900.00
WURLITZER 24. 1938.
78, 24 selections. 3500.00

NOT SHOWN —
WURLITZER 1650. 1953/54.
45, 48 selections. $2500.00

SEEBURG 100C. 1952.
45, 50 records, 100 selections.
. . . . $4700.00

SEEBURG 161. Select-O-Matic.
1958. 45, first year with 80
records, 160 selections. $5100.00

AMI Model C. 1950.
78, 20 records, 40 selections.
. . . . $4100.00

ROCK-OLA WALLBOX. 1950's.
120 selections. $135.00

ROCK-OLA CAPRI II 414S. 1964.
Sterio/Mono . 45, 50 records,
100 selections. $1600.00

ROCK-OLA 443. 1969/70.
Stereo/Mono. 50 records,
100 selections. $1500.00

SEWING COLLECTABLES

Left —
EIGHT SPOOL CAROUSEL
THREAD HOLDER.
With pin cushion.
1920's.
Ht. 3" $35.00

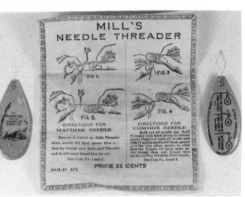

NEEDLE THREADERS. Prudential
Insurance Co. advertising on one
side with instructions on reverse.
Ca. 1920's.
Complete with envelope. $12.00

RED CLOTH STRAWBERRIES.
Contain sand, used to polish
needles. L. 1½"
Each $10.00

SOCK DARNERS.
Top — 1920's. Length 4" $15.00
Bottom — 1940's. Length 6" 20.00

PIN CUSHIONS. All mid-1940's. Left to Right —
"FRAE BONNIE SCOTLAND" Ht. 3" $10.00
TEAPOT. Ht. 2" 12.00
LION. 20.00

METAL SHOE PIN CUSHIONS. Ca. 1900 - 1910.
Left—L. 4" $30.00. Upper Right—L. 3" $25.00. Lower Right—L.3½" $20.00

Left to Right —
BARREL THIMBLE HOLDER. Ca. 1920. L. 2" $12.00
ACORN THIMBLE HOLDER. Ca. 1940. L. 1¾" 40.00
SHOES. One thimble holder, one pin cushion. Ca. 1950. L. 2¼" Ea. 20.00

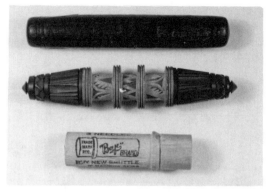

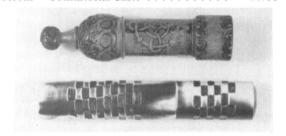

NEEDLE CASES.
Top — Wood. Length 4" $20.00
Middle — Carved Wood. 75.00
Bottom — Commercial Case. 20.00

SEWING KITS.
Blue enamel case,
gilt thimble and
2 spools.
L. 2" $22.00

Yellow enamel with
Eastern Star insignia,
2 spools.
L. 2" 25.00

NEEDLE CASES. With threaded caps.
Top — Carved and coloured. From India $30.00
Bottom — Coloured celluloid. French. L. 3½" 30.00

LADIES COMPANION: Tiny sewing
kit (illus. above, left) with thimble cap
containing thread and sewing needles.
Kits of this type were carried by many
soldiers during World War 1.

Left —
CERAMIC CAT.
Made in Japan, 1930's.
Tape measure in base, pin
cushion hat, hole above
nose for thimble.
Ht. 6" $10.00

257

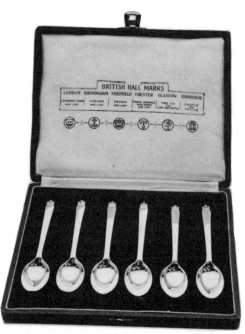

SILVER

ROYAL
COMMEMORATIVE
Coronation, Elizabeth II
June 2, 1953

Set of six sterling teaspoons in silk and velvet lined case, each spoon bearing the mark of the assay office. $350.00

Hallmarks on spoons illustrated above.
Symbols indicate the maker's mark, standard mark (sterling), assay office mark (town), year mark and Monarch.

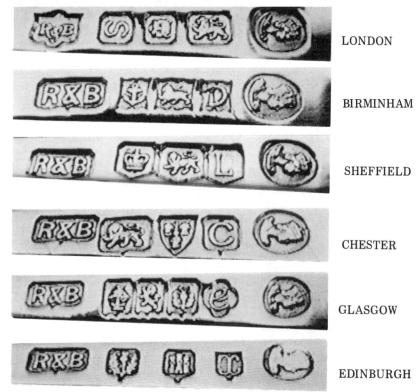

LONDON

BIRMINHAM

SHEFFIELD

CHESTER

GLASGOW

EDINBURGH

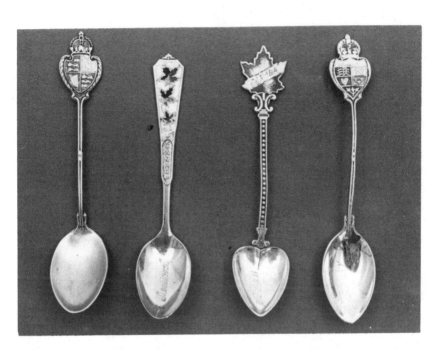

SOUVENIR SPOONS. Sterling.
Above — Left to Right —

ROYAL COAT OF
ARMS. $35.00

MONTREAL,
QUEBEC 40.00

MIDLAND,
ONTARIO 40.00

SUDBURY,
ONTARIO 35.00

SOUVENIR SPOONS. Sterling.

Left —
TRAIL,
BRITISH COLUMBIA $150.00

Right —
CANADIAN COAT
OF ARMS 65.00

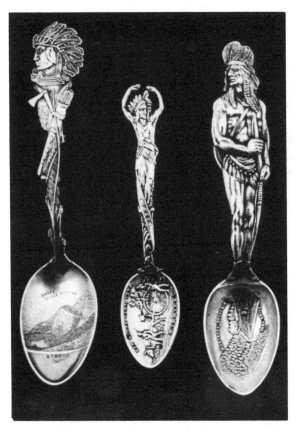

SOUVENIR SPOONS.
Sterling.
Left to Right —

ALBERTA . . $175.00

WINNIPEG,
MANITOBA   145.00

MONTREAL,
QUEBEC   200.00

SOUVENIR SPOONS. Silverplate with enamel.

Above — Vancouver, British Columbia $40.00
Below — Canada 25.00

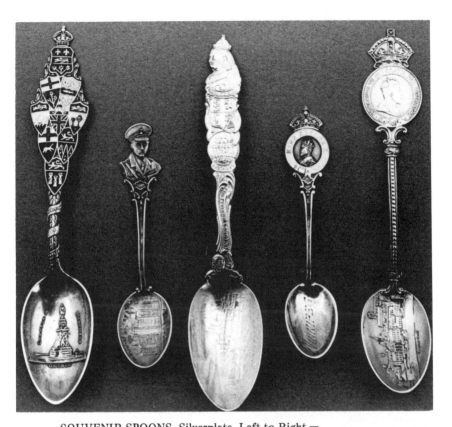

SOUVENIR SPOONS. Silverplate. Left to Right —
Dominion of Canada. $75.00
Edward VIII 40.00
Queen Victoria Diamond Jubilee 55.00
George VI 40.00
Edward VII 45.00

SOUVENIR SPOON. Silverplate. George V and Queen Mary
Silver Jubilee. $50.00

SOUVENIR SPOON. Silverplate. George VI and Queen Elizabeth Coronation. $45.00

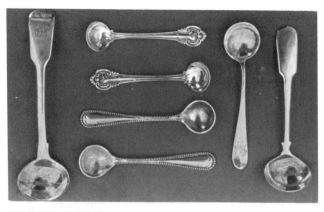

STERLING SALT SPOONS.
Left — London Mark, 1827. L. 4" $35.00
Top — Marked "Sterling" L. 2½" Pair 35.00
Bottom — Roden Bros. Toronto. Pair 40.00
Right — Birmingham mark, 1895. L. 3" 30.00
        London mark, 1826. L. 3½" 45.00

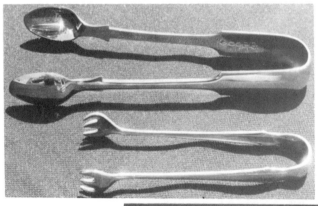

SUGAR TONGS.
Top — Silverplate, English,
L. 5½" .. $35.00
Bottom — Sterling.
International Silver Co. L. 4"   60.00

Top — Berry Spoon.
1847 Rogers Triple Plate. L. 9" $ 28.00
Centre — Sterling Parfait Spoon.
Ca. 1900.
L. 8½" 35.00
Bottom — Sterling Serving Spoon.
London mark, 1802.
L. 9"   .. 100.00

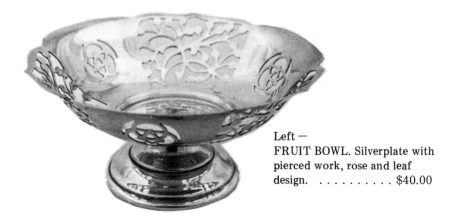

Left —
FRUIT BOWL. Silverplate with pierced work, rose and leaf design. $40.00

BUTTER DISH. Quadruple plate. Revolving cover, clear glass liner, sterling knife. $150.00

SARDINE BOX. Clear glass dish, silverplate lid in silverplate frame. 6¼" x 5" x 5" $135.00

Left — BAKING SERVING DISH. Meriden Quadruple Plate, Ca. 1870. Diam. 12" $120.00

TEA SERVICE. Silverplate, by Roden Bros., Toronto. Ca. 1900.
Teapot 6½" high $350.00

TEA SERVICE. Silverplate, by J. Deakin & Sons, Sheffield, England.
Ca. 1900. Teapot 6¼" high. $310.00

TEA SERVICE. Silverplate, marked Made in England. Ca. 1900.
Teapot 5½" high. $295.00

CANDLESTICKS. Silverplate.
Ca. 1890. Ht. 10½"
Pair $465.00

CANDLESTICKS. Silverplate.
Ca. 1890. Ht. 7¾"
Pair $415.00

CALLING CARD RECEIVER.
Silverplate, by Standard Silver
Plate Co., Toronto.
Ca. 1890. . . . . $95.00

CALLING CARD RECEIVER.
Meriden Silver Plate frame with
decorated black glass insert.
Ca. 1880. . . . . . . $135.00

TOYS

MAMOD STEAM CAR. Made in England. Rubber tires. L. 15"
1960's. Never used, mint in box. $350.00

MAMOD STEAM ROLLER & TRAILER. Made in England.
Both 10" long. 1960's. Never used, mint in box. . . $350.00

MAMOD STEAM TRACTOR & TRAILER. Made in England.
Tractor, 10" long. Trailer, 12" long. 1960's. Never used,
mint in box. $350.00

Left —
WIND-UP EISTLER CAR.
Made in U.S. Zone, Germany,
1946 - 52.
L. 10" $250.00

Right —
WIND-UP EISTLER CAR.
Made in U.S. Zone, Germany,
1946 -52.
L. 10" $250.00

Left —
WIND-UP SCHUCO CAR.
Made in U.S. Zone, Germany.
1946 - 52. . . . . . . $140.00

Right —
WIND-UP SCHUCO CAR.
Made in U.S. Zone, Germany.
1946 - 52. . . . . . . $150.00

Left —
WIND-UP SCHUCO RACING
CAR. Made in U.S. Zone,
Germany, 1946 -52 $175.00

Right —
WIND-UP MARX MARVEL
CAR. Made in U.S.A.
1938. L. 15" $275.00

Left —
WIND-UP MODEL OF SCARAB
CAR. By Buddy L, 1935.
L. 10½" Mint. $225.00

The Scarab, was made in 1935,
to sell for $5000.00. It was too
expensive and didn't sell.

Right —
WIND-UP SIREN FIRE
CHIEF. By Marx. With
battery operated siren
and lights. 1934. L. 11½"
Fair condition. $275.00

Right —
FRICTION GUN BOAT.
Made in U.S.A. for Sears.
1921.
L. 15" $550.00

Left —
WIND-UP BOAT. West
Germany, 1950's.
L. 10½"
With box.   . . $135.00

WIND-UP. By Arnold,
Germany, made for Sears,
1950's.
Left —
TUG BOAT. L. 12"
With box. $275.00
Right —
LINER. L. 12"
With box. 275.00

Left —
SUBMARINE.
Japanese, 1950's.
L. 15" $165.00

Left —
DOUGHBOY CLOCKWORK
TANK. By Marx. Soldier pops
up as toy moves along. L. 10"
1940 - 50.
Good condition. . . $250.00

Right —
WIND-UP TANK. By Marx.
With rubber tracks, emits
sparks as it runs. L. 9½"
1940 - 50. . . . . $235.00

Left —
FRICTION POLICE
MOTORCYCLE. Litho-tin.
Japanese, 1950's.
Mint $75.00

Right —
FRICTION MOTORCYCLE
& RIDER. Litho-tin. West
German, 1950's.
Mint. $100.00

JEU DE COURSE. French, lever operated betting game, horse and jockeys rotate. Wood box 11" square. 1890 - 1910. Good condition. $1700.00

NOT SHOWN —
WIND-UP SKY HAWK AIRPLANE. By Marx, Ca. 1930's. Planes on wire circle tower. Ht. 8" Span 19" $82.00

NOT SHOWN —
BUCKET. Litho-tin with Disney characters. The Ohio Art Co., 1938. . . . . $170.00
RING TOSS GAME. Wood, Felix The Cat. Ca. 1935. . . 55.00
SHOOFLY ROCKER. 235.00

WIND-UP JOY RIDE. German, late 1940's. Ht. 8" Not working. $125.00

SAND BOX TOY. Sandy & Andy, made in the U.S.A. 1920's. Activated by pouring sand in hopper. Ht. 7" Good condition. $125.00

THE DRUMMING CLOWN —
CHARLIE. By Alps, Japan, mid
1950's. Plays drum, red nose
lights up. $145.00

PLAYBOY. By Cragston, Japan,
early 1960's. Cloth and rubber on
tin box. He drinks and spins round
and round. Ht. 14"
Working $165.00

JUMBO THE BUBBLE BLOWING
ELEPHANT. By Y Co., Japan, late
1950's. Working, complete with
box. Ht. 8" $150.00

MR. McPOOCH. By The San Co.,
Japan, Ca. 1953. Brown dog, plaid
jacket. He walks, inhales on pipe
and blows smoke. $150.00

WIND-UP MOTOR BOAT. By Haji, Japan. Red, white and blue, on trailer. Length 7"
Working model $65.00

WIND-UP AIRPLANE ON TOWER. German, by Bing, Ca. 1926. Red and green tower, silver plane. Tower 10" high. $595.00

WADDLES FAMILY CAR. By Y Co., Japan, 1950's. Ht. 6½" L. 6½" $135.00

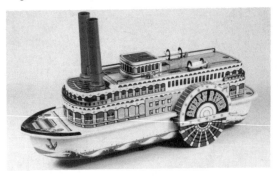

BATTERY OPERATED PADDLE WHEELER. By Modern Toys, Japan. L. 12½.. Early 1960's. $150.00

SCOTTIE DOG BANKS. Hard plastic, by Reliable, Canada. Ht. 7½" Ca. 1950's.   Each $20.00

Right —
LUNCH BOX. Litho tin.
"Jiminy Cricket says —
Stop, Look & Listen"
Ht. 4½"
Length 7" $60.00

PINOCCHIO HAND PUPPET.
Celluloid head, 1940's.
Ht. 10" $35.00

WIND-UP WALKING BEAR. Made in Japan, no maker's name, mid 1950's. Black, yellow plastic eyes.
Ht. 6" $85.00

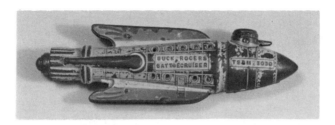

BUCK ROGERS BATTLE CRUISER. Gray and blue painted alloy. Has pulley inside, slides down a string held at an angle. 1938. Length 4½" $125.00

"SUN VALLEY" SKI JUMPER. By Wolverine, Ca. 1940's. Wood, litho card and metal. Spring action flips skier at end of run. Length 26" $75.00

STEAM ENGINE & ATTACHMENTS. By Wilesco, 1940's.
Left to Right —
TRIPLE STEAM HAMMER. .... $ 35.00
ENGINE WITH GOVERNOR 100.00
COLOUR EFFECT TOY 25.00
VERTICAL DRILL 50.00

HALLOWEEN PUMPKIN. Litho tin, orange, yellow and black, cut-out face. 1940's. Ht. 5" Front and back views $45.00

DISNEY FIGURES, Minnie Mouse, Scrooge McDuck, Donald Duck and Goofy. Alloy, made from a home casting set. Ht. 3½" to 4" 1940's. Each $25.00

CHILD'S WHISTLE/RATTLE.
Embossed "For a good child"
Length 7" $25.00

SEWING MACHINE.
Casige, British Zone,
Germany, 1946 - 52.
Length 6½" $45.00

Right —
PHONOGRAPH.
Made in U.S.A. Gold
colour sound box, yellow
tone arm.
Ht. 5"
Length 8" $225.00

Left —
THE "CRESCENT"
Cast iron stove with
removeable lids and
shelves.
Back 7½" high
Length 10" $130.00

"CARRYING THE TOOLS TO BRITAIN" Full colour board game, 36" x 14" Ca. 1940. A Canadian Broadcasting Corporation promotion to sell War Bonds. $35.00

Left —
AMERICAN FLYER
STOCK CAR RACE,
No. 19060 by
A.C. Gilbert Co.,
Newhaven, Conn.
Mid 1950's. Complete
in full colour box.
16" x 18" . . $150.00

"MOVIE COMICS" VIEWER, by the Cheerio Co., Canada, early 1940's. With 22 comic strip films and 2 boxes of parts. (Illustrated — Terry and the Pirates, Little Orphan Annie, Dick Tracy and The Lone Ranger. Set $175.00

INDEX

CERAMICS

PRESSED GLASS

TOYS

CLOCK HOUSE COLLECTOR BOOKS

"UNITT'S CANADIAN PRICE GUIDE TO ANTIQUES & COLLECTABLES"
BOOK 10 (1984) $16.95, BOOK 13 (1990) $16.95, BOOK 14 (1991)
1-55041-0253 $16.95
The guide with prices and photographs gathered from the Canadian market-place......each guide is illustrated throughout with new photographs of antiques and collectables for sale at antique stores, shows, sales, etc.
"UNITT'S BOOK OF MARKS ON ANTIQUES & COLLECTABLES"
1-55041-027X Revised and Expanded $16.95
Contains maker's marks on antiques, such as Canadian silversmiths' marks; British Hall marks; Silverplate marks of Canadian manufacturers; marks on art glass; cut glass; bottles, etc; ceramics; china; pottery and porcelain.
"UNITT'S BOTTLES & VALUES & MORE" 1-55041-0172 $16.95
Articles and information about methods of bottle making and Canadian manufacturers. Hundreds of bottles illustrated and priced.
"UNITT'S CANADIAN PRICE GUIDE TO DOLLS & TOYS" Revised
1-55041-0296 $16.95
This guide shows Canadian dolls, their makers and marks; European and American dolls are included. Doll furniture and accessories are illustrated. Various types of toys are shown and priced.
"PETER'S CLOCK BOOK" 0-919134-017 $9.95
Illustrated step-by-step guide to cleaning spring-or weight-driven clocks......plus hints on restoring cases.
"CANADIAN HANDBOOK OF PRESSED GLASS TABLEWARE"
0-919134-009 $35.00
An essential reference book. Direct and concise information on Canadian pressed glass with 600 black and white photographs of over 230 patterns. Factories, alternate names, and forms known are listed with each pattern.
"AMERICAN & CANADIAN GOBLETS" Volume I 0-919134-092 $39.95
Over 1,000 Canadian and American goblets are illustrated, cross-referenced, and indexed in this well received book. A most comprehensive work on the subject having many examples not previously shown.
CATALOGUE REPRINTS — Primary source material such as reprints of Canadian manufacturers' catalogues are a valuable research aid to collectors.
"TORONTO SILVERPLATE CO., 1888 CATALOGUE" 0-919134-05X $14.95
......illustrates and gives original prices for plated articles made by this firm.
More Fitzhenry & Whiteside titles:
"HOW TO RESTORE AND REPAIR PRACTICALLY EVERYTHING"
Revised Edition by Lorraine Johnson 0-7181-30448 $19.95
Superbly illustrated guide to restoration; an indispensable source of information ranging from restoring stained-glass panels to rethreading pearls.
Funk & Wagnalls CANADIAN COLLEGE DICTIONARY, indexed
0-88902-9237 $29.95
"The best of the lot for our purposes in Canada" — W.E. Messenger, Professor of English, University of British Columbia.
"READ FOR YOUR LIFE" 1-55041-051-2 $16.95
Both a psychological self-help book and a testimonial to literature. Sections on reading for the elderly, for adolescents, for children and adults. Reading during crises, bereavement, divorce; for woman, disabled, and minorities.

For a current list of our books for collectors, write to:
Fitzhenry & Whiteside
195 Allstate Parkway
Markham, Ont. L3R 4T8